**Teacher's Edition**

# WORKBOOK

## HARCOURT SCIENCE

Seth

### Harcourt School Publishers

Orlando • Boston • Dallas • Chicago • San Diego

www.harcourtschool.com

## REPRODUCING COPIES FOR STUDENTS

This Teacher's Edition contains full-size student pages with answers printed in non-reproducible blue ink.

It may be necessary to adjust the exposure control on your photocopy machine to a lighter setting to ensure that blue answers do not reproduce.

# Contents

# Reading in Science

Reading is very important in your becoming an independent learner—in being able to find, understand, and apply the information you need in the classroom and in your life. In science reading you are expected to find information, learn the meanings of scientific words, and put together ideas and observations. You can be helped in this reading and understanding by using the following suggestions.

To help you locate topics in *Harcourt Science* and most other science texts, use the:

- table of contents,
- titles of units, chapters, and lessons,
- headings and subheadings,
- index.

Look for and read these parts of a lesson in *Harcourt Science* to locate main ideas and other key information:

- Vocabulary Preview
- Investigate activity
- Process Skill Tip
- Find Out
- ✓ questions
- Picture captions
- Inside Story
- Summary
- Review
- Links
- Features

To help you recognize and read for specific kinds of information:

1. Recognize the text structure by looking for signal words
   - compare/contrast—*however, but, some, different, instead, on the other hand, like, unlike, both, neither*
   - sequence or how-to—*first, second, next, then, last, finally,* or the use of numbered steps
   - cause/effect—*since, because, as a result*

2. Preview the material to see at a glance which material you already know something about and which contains new or unfamiliar topics.

3. First, read the questions at the end of a lesson or chapter. Then read the lesson or chapter to find the answers. Also use the **Find Out** statements to help you identify what you need to find out while reading.

4. Construct graphic organizers or use the graphic organizers provided in the workbook to help you remember key points as you read.

5. Read the Science **Process Skill Tip** in each investigation to help you understand the meaning of a process skill. Do the Process Skill Practice page in the workbook for more information.

6. Write a summary of the main ideas of a lesson. Put in your own words (paraphrase) what you read about. Then compare your summary to the lesson summary in the book.

7. Look for comparison words such as *like* or *similar to*. These words can help you to understand something new by comparing it to something you already know about.

8. Read the entire sentence and sometimes the sentences around highlighted vocabulary to tell you what these words mean.

9. Make an outline of what you read to record main points.

10. Ask questions as you read. Write facts in one column on a sheet of paper. Write your questions in the column next to the facts.

11. Reflect on what you read. Write notes not only about what you read, but also about what you think, and why.

12. Use the **Review** in the text and the **Concept Review** and **Vocabulary Review** in the workbook to help you prepare for the chapter test.

# Chapter 1 • Graphic Organizer for Chapter Concepts

## From Single Cells to Body Systems

Name _____

Date _____

# Observing Cells

## Materials

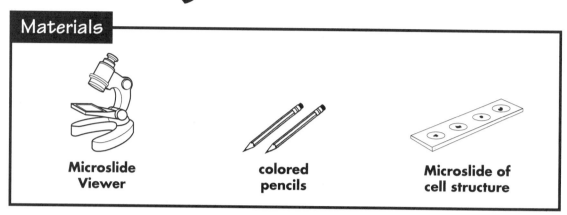

Microslide Viewer

colored pencils

Microslide of cell structure

## Alternate Materials

slice of onion

coverslip

red food coloring

colored pencils

microscope slide

dropper

microscope

## Activity Procedure

1. Insert the Cell Structure Microslide in the slot on the Microslide Viewer. Turn the focus knob until you can see the cells clearly.

2. **Observe** the onion skin cells and the human cheek cells. **Record** your observations by using the colored pencils to make drawings.

3. Now **observe** the green leaf cells and the nerve cells. Again, **record** your observations by making drawings.

4. Now **compare** your drawings. Make a Venn diagram with two large, overlapping circles. Label the circles *Plant Cells* and *Animal Cells*. Label the area where the circles overlap *Both Cells*. Draw the cell parts that you **observed** in the proper circles. Leave enough room to label the parts as you read about them in this lesson.

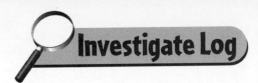

## Draw Conclusions

**1. Compare** the outer layers of plant and animal cells. The plant cells have a
thick outer "wall," while the outer layer of the animal cells is much thinner.

_____

**2.** In the centers of most cells are structures that control the cells' activities.
How many of these structures are there in each of the cells you **observed**?
one _____

**3. Scientists at Work** Scientists often **infer** characteristics of a group of objects
by **observing** just a few of the objects. From your observations, what do you
infer about the number of controlling structures in a cell? Every cell has a
single controlling structure.

_____

**Investigate Further** Now that you have **observed** photomicrographs of cells,
use the materials in the *Alternate Materials* list to observe living cells from
onion skin. Then **compare** your observations with the drawings you made in
this investigation. See page R5 for tips on using a microscope.

_____

_____

_____

_____

_____

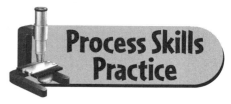

# Observe and Infer

Observing is the most basic science skill. Making good observations will allow you to develop other important science skills, like inferring, comparing, classifying, and measuring. Inferring involves the use of logical reasoning to make conclusions based on observations. Inferences are explanations for events, are based on judgments, and are not always correct.

## Think About Observing and Inferring

You looked at cells during the investigation for this lesson. Imagine you come to class and find that all the microscope slides have been removed from their holders and had their labels removed. Use your observations and your knowledge of cells to answer the following questions and make inferences.

1. Your teacher asks you and other students to help relabel the slides by separating the cell slides from the other slides. What do you need to look

    for to decide whether or not you are looking at a cell slide? _____

    _____

    _____

2. Next your teacher asks you to separate the plant cell slides from the animal cell slides. What do you need to look for to decide whether or not you are looking

    at a plant cell slide or an animal cell slide? _____

    _____

    _____

3. What would you look for to decide whether you were seeing that structure?

    _____

    _____

4. What inference could you make about why such a difference is found in plant

    and animal cells? _____

    _____

Name _____

Date _____

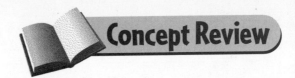

# What Are Cells, and What Do They Do?

## Lesson Concept

Living things are made of one or more cells, each able to support the functions of life. Plant cells differ from animal cells in that they have cell walls and chloroplasts.

## Vocabulary

| | | |
|---|---|---|
| **cell** (A6) | **cell membrane** (A8) | **nucleus** (A8) |
| **cytoplasm** (A9) | **diffusion** (A10) | **osmosis** (A10) |
| **tissue** (A12) | **organ** (A12) | **system** (A12) |

**Match the name of each structure or process with its function.**

___D___ **1.** muscle tissue

___G___ **2.** chromosomes

___A___ **3.** passive transport

___F___ **4.** diffusion

___H___ **5.** nervous tissue

___J___ **6.** active transport

___B___ **7.** chloroplasts

___E___ **8.** cell membrane

___I___ **9.** nucleus

___C___ **10.** vacuoles

**A** energy-free movement of materials through a cell membrane

**B** make food in plant cells

**C** store food, water, and waste materials for the cell

**D** can move an animal's skeleton by contracting and relaxing

**E** holds parts of the cell together and separates the cell from its surroundings

**F** the way most materials move in and out of cells

**G** threadlike structures that contain information about the characteristics of the organism

**H** carries electrical signals that affect muscle tissue

**I** controls the cell's activities

**J** use of a carrier and energy from a cell to transport materials through the cell

Name _____

Date _____

# Cells and Tissues

## Materials

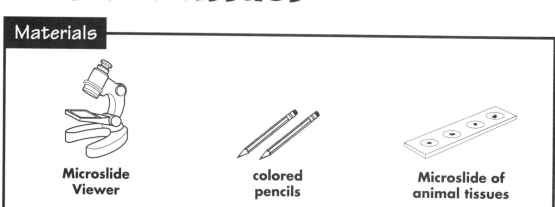

**Microslide Viewer**

**colored pencils**

**Microslide of animal tissues**

## Alternate Materials

**prepared slides of epithelial, connective, and nervous tissues**

**microscope**

## Activity Procedure

**1** Insert the Animal Tissues Microslide in the slot of the Microslide Viewer. Turn the focus knob until you can see the cells and tissues clearly.

**2** **Observe** the voluntary muscle cells. **Record** your observations by using the colored pencils to make a drawing. Label your drawing with the name of the tissue. Then describe the tissue. You may use the Microslide text folder to help you write your description.

**3** Repeat Step 2 for the smooth muscle cells and the heart muscle.

**4** **Compare** the three kinds of muscle tissue.

Name _____

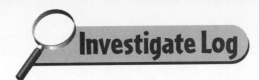 

## Draw Conclusions

**1.** The muscle tissue cells all have a nucleus and mitochondria. How are the three kinds of muscle tissue alike? How are they different?

The voluntary muscle tissue has long, thin cells. The cells of the smooth

muscle tissue were shorter and more tightly packed. Cells of the heart

muscle seemed to be interconnected.

**2.** The dark-stained organelles you **observed** in the muscle tissues are mitochondria. Which kind of muscle tissue has the most mitochondria?

heart muscle

**3. Scientists at Work** When scientists **compare** objects, they often **infer** reasons for any differences. What do you infer about why one kind of muscle tissue has more mitochondria than the others? Since the heart is always beating, heart

tissue needs more energy than other muscle tissue.

**Investigate Further** Now that you have **observed** several kinds of tissues, use the materials in the *Alternate Materials* list to study other kinds of tissue. Observe the tissues under the microscope, and draw what you see. **Compare** these tissues with the muscle tissues you observed. See page R4 for tips on using a microscope.

Students should note that the cells making up each of the other tissues

look different from the cells of the muscle tissue but still have the same

basic cell parts.

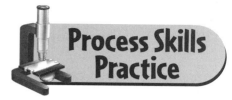

# Compare and Infer

When you compare data, you arrange your information so that you can see similarities and differences. Inferring involves the use of logical reasoning to make conclusions based on observations.

## Think About Comparing and Inferring

Rajean was doing a comparative study to test a new preservative. She made a nutrient solution for microorganisms from beef broth. Then she put 100 mL of the broth in three different beakers. She put 0.1 mL of the preservative in *Beaker A*, 0.01 mL in *Beaker B*, and 0.001 mL in *Beaker C*. The next day Rajean checked the beakers and found the broth discolored and cloudy in two of them. So, she used a microscope to check a sample from each of the three beakers. She recorded what she observed.

|  | Beaker A | Beaker B | Beaker C |
|---|---|---|---|
| Amount of preservative added to beaker | 0.1 mL | 0.01 mL | 0.001 mL |
| Appearance of broth | Clear | Somewhat cloudy | Very cloudy |
| Microorganisms seen under microscope | None | Yeast cells | Yeast and bacteria |

1. Compare the mixtures in each beaker. How are they different?

   _____

2. How are they alike? _____

   _____

3. After 24 hours, how do the beakers compare? _____

   _____

4. What can you infer about how effective the preservative is in keeping yeast

   from growing in the solution? _____

   _____

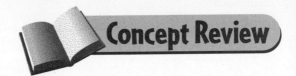
Concept Review

# How Are Human Body Systems Organized?

## Lesson Concept

Body cells are organized into tissues, organs, and systems that work together to keep the body alive. Four of the major systems are the circulatory, the respiratory, the digestive, and the excretory.

## Vocabulary

**capillaries** (A17)   **alveoli** (A18)   **villi** (A19)   **nephrons** (A20)

**Match the name of each structure or process with its function.**

_C_ **1.** circulatory system

_H_ **2.** platelets

_K_ **3.** alveoli

_B_ **4.** esophagus

_A_ **5.** capillaries

_D_ **6.** ureters

_J_ **7.** trachea

_E_ **8.** arteries

_G_ **9.** heart

_F_ **10.** saliva

_L_ **11.** pancreas

_I_ **12.** sweating

**A** blood vessels so small that blood cells have to move through them in single file

**B** a long tube that leads to the stomach

**C** transports oxygen, nutrients, and wastes through the body in the blood

**D** tubes that empty wastes into the bladder from the kidneys

**E** vessels through which blood leaves the heart

**F** moistens food and begins to break down starchy foods

**G** pumps blood through blood vessels

**H** cause blood to clot when a blood vessel is cut

**I** eliminates excess body heat

**J** sometimes called the windpipe

**K** tiny air sacs in the lungs

**L** produces a fluid that neutralizes stomach acid

# How Muscles Cause Movement

## Materials

tape measure

## Activity Procedure

**1** Place your left hand on top of your right arm, between the shoulder and elbow. Bend and straighten your right arm at the elbow. **Observe** the movement by feeling the muscles in your right arm.

**2** The muscle on the front of the upper arm is called the *biceps*. The muscle on the back of the upper arm is called the *triceps*. **Compare** the biceps and the triceps as you bend and straighten your arm. **Infer** which muscle controls the bending movement and which controls the straightening movement.

**3** Have a partner use the tape measure to **measure** the distance around your upper arm when it is straight and when it is bent. **Record** the measurements.

**4** Repeat Steps 2 and 3, using your right hand and your left arm.

**5** **Compare** the sets of measurements.

Name _____

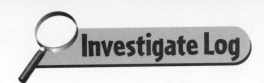 

## Draw Conclusions

1. What did you **infer** about the muscles controlling the bending and the straightening of your upper arm? The biceps bends the arm, and the triceps straightens it.

2. Why are two muscles needed to bend and straighten your arm? Why can't one muscle do it? A muscle only works "one way"; it can only contract to move a bone in one direction.

3. **Scientists at Work** Scientists often **hypothesize** about things they **observe**. Hypothesize about any differences between the measurements of your right arm and the measurements of your left arm. Students might hypothesize that the arm that does more work has larger muscles.

**Investigate Further** Repeat the investigation with different pairs of muscles. Try bending your leg at the knee while **observing** the muscles in your thigh. See if these observations also support your hypothesis. _____

# Hypothesize

When you hypothesize, you make an educated guess about the results of an experiment you plan to do. A hypothesis is based upon observation, prior knowledge, and prior experimental outcomes. A hypothesis is often altered based on the outcome of experiments that test it.

## Think About Hypothesizing

A group of students decided to test the effect of sleep and repeated trials on reaction time. Their hypothesis was that reaction time would improve with more sleep and repeated trials. Each student in the test was asked to push a button as soon as he or she heard the sound of a bell. The amount of time between the sound of the bell and the pushing of the button was recorded as the reaction time.

The table below lists reaction times for three students on different days after receiving different amounts of sleep the night before. Each student underwent two trials on each day of testing.

| Amount of Sleep | Reaction Time in Seconds | | | | | |
| | Student A | | Student B | | Student C | |
| | Trial 1 | Trial 2 | Trial 1 | Trial 2 | Trial 1 | Trial 2 |
| --- | --- | --- | --- | --- | --- | --- |
| 8 hours | 0.20 | 0.16 | 0.15 | 0.12 | 0.25 | 0.19 |
| 6 hours | 0.17 | 0.17 | 0.19 | 0.24 | 0.25 | 0.32 |
| 4 hours | 0.30 | 0.45 | 0.35 | 0.47 | 0.40 | 0.45 |
| 2 hours | 0.82 | 1.10 | 0.75 | 1.08 | 0.80 | 1.02 |

**1.** Was the hypothesis correct? _____

**2.** Use the data to form a hypothesis about the effect of sleeping less than eight hours a night on reaction time. _____

_____

_____

**3.** How would you test this hypothesis? _____

_____

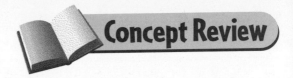

Concept Review

# How Do Bones, Muscles, and Nerves Work Together?

## Lesson Concept

Skeletal bones move because of the action of pairs of voluntary muscles. Smooth muscles line digestive organs and blood vessels. The walls of the heart are made of cardiac muscle. Nerves carry signals from sensory organs to the brain and from the brain to the muscles.

## Vocabulary

**bone marrow** (A24)        **joints** (A24)        **tendons** (A25)

**ligaments** (A25)        **neuron** (A26)        **receptors** (A26)

**Match the term in the left column with its description in the right column.**

_G_ **1.** bone marrow

_J_ **2.** ligaments

_E_ **3.** tendons

_A_ **4.** smooth muscles

_H_ **5.** cardiac muscles

_L_ **6.** joints

_B_ **7.** central nervous system

_D_ **8.** receptors

_K_ **9.** neurons

_F_ **10.** dendrites

_C_ **11.** axon

_I_ **12.** synapse

**A** line digestive organs and blood vessels

**B** is made up of the brain and the spinal cord

**C** is the part of the neuron that carries signals and transmits them to other neurons

**D** are nerve cells that detect conditions in the body's environment

**E** attach bones to muscles

**F** branch out of the nerve cell and receive signals from other cells

**G** produces red and white blood cells

**H** make up the walls of the heart

**I** is a gap between the axon of one neuron and the dendrite of the next neuron

**J** attach bones to each other

**K** are the cells that nerves are made of

**L** are where the bones meet to attach to each other and to muscles

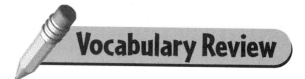

# Recognize Vocabulary

Listed below are scrambled vocabulary terms from Chapter 1. Use the clues to unscramble the terms. Write the unscrambled terms on the lines provided.

**1.** S M O O S S I  _____
the movement of water and dissolved materials through cell membranes

**2.** L L R C A S E I A P I  _____
blood vessels so small that blood cells move through them in single file

**3.** R U N N E O  _____
a specialized cell that can receive and transmit signals to other cells like it

**4.** L Y M O C P S T A  _____
a jellylike substance containing chemicals that keep the cell functioning

**5.** G R O A N  _____
tissues that work together form this

**6.** L C L E  _____
the basic unit of structure and function of all living things

**7.** J S T O N I  _____
where bones meet and are attached to each other and to muscles

**8.** P R E E T O C R S  _____
nerve cells that detect conditions in the body's environment

**9.** I I L V L  _____
tiny tubes sticking out from the walls of the small intestine

**10.** O M N O E A W B R R (2 words)  _____
connective tissue that produces red and white blood cells

**11.** F D N I U F I O S  _____
the way most materials move in and out of cells

**12.** M C L N E E M E R L B A (2 words)  _____
a thin covering that encloses a cell

**13.** I G L E S A N T M  _____
bands of connective tissue that hold the skeleton together

**14.** V I O A L E L  _____
tiny air sacs at the end of the smallest tubes in the lungs

Chapter 2 • Graphic Organizer for Chapter Concepts

## Animal Growth and Reproduction

Name _____

Date _____

# Cell Reproduction

## Materials

**Microslide Viewer**

**Microslide of plant mitosis**

**Microslide of animal mitosis**

## Alternate Materials

**microscope**

**prepared slides of plant cells dividing**

**prepared slides of animal cells dividing**

## Activity Procedure

**1** Insert the Plant Mitosis Microslide into the slot in the Microslide Viewer. Turn the focus knob until you can see the cells clearly.

**2** **Observe** the plant cells dividing. **Record** what you observe in each stage of cell division. The descriptions on the Microslide card may help you. Then draw pictures of what you see at each stage.

**3** Now insert the Animal Mitosis Microslide into the slot of the Microslide Viewer. Again turn the focus knob until you can see the cells clearly.

**4** **Observe** the animal cells dividing. **Record** what you observe in each stage of cell division. Again you may use the descriptions on the Microslide card to help you. Then draw pictures of what you see at each stage.

**5** Now **compare** the stages of plant cell division with the stages of animal cell division. How are the stages alike? How are they different? **Record** your observations.

Name _____

## Draw Conclusions

**1.** What part of the cell changes as cell division occurs? What changes take place?
The nucleus; in some cells the nucleus disappears, cross-shaped structures
line up in the center of some cells, and some cells look as if they are splitting
into two cells.

**2.** How many new cells does each dividing cell produce? two

**3.** What similarities and differences did you **observe** between the dividing plant
cells and the dividing animal cells? Possible answers: Both plant and
animal cells had a visible nucleus, materials inside the nucleus divided in
both, and the stages of cell division were the same in both. The plant cells
had cell walls and the animal cells did not.

**4. Scientists at Work** Scientists **observe** cells and ask questions based on their
observations. What questions do you have about cell division, based on what
you observed? Questions will vary.

_____

_____

**Investigate Further** Now that you have **observed** photomicrographs of plant and
animal cells dividing, use the materials on the *Alternate Materials* list to observe
other cells dividing. See page R4 for tips on using a microscope.

_____

_____

_____

Name _____

Date _____

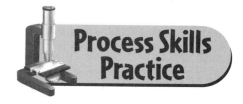

# Observe

Observing is the most basic science skill. Making good observations will allow you to develop other important skills, such as comparing and classifying.

## Think About Observing

Do all plant cells look alike? Do all animal cells look alike? Observe the drawings below, and compare them to what you know about cells. Then classify them by writing *plant* or *animal* beneath the drawing.

**1.** What observation can you make to determine which cells are plant cells?

_____

**2.** Do you observe anything unusual about one of the plant cells and one of the animal cells? _____

_____

4. _____

3. _____

5. _____

6. _____

7. _____

**Use with page A37.**

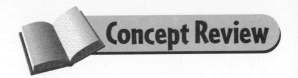
Concept Review

# Growth and Reproduction

## Lesson Concept

Organisms grow when their cells divide. Body cells divide through mitosis. Reproductive cells divide through meiosis.

## Vocabulary

| | | |
|---|---|---|
| **chromosome** (A39) | **mitosis** (A39) | **asexual reproduction** (A41) |
| **sexual reproduction** (A42) | **meiosis** (A42) | |

Use the terms from the box to fill in the blanks in the paragraph that follows. Watch out! One term is used twice.

| | | |
|---|---|---|
| **sexual reproduction** | **regenerate** | **planaria** |
| **mitosis** | **meiosis** | **zygote** |
| **asexual reproduction** | **chromosomes** | **planarian** |

Organisms grow when their cells divide in a process called _____mitosis_____.

To prepare for this process, a cell makes copies of its _____chromosomes_____. After this process, each of the new cells has an exact copy of the original cell's

_____chromosomes_____. When a cut or scrape on your skin heals, it is because this

process of cell division has allowed the damaged tissue to _____regenerate_____.

The freshwater flatworm, called a _____planarian_____, can regenerate most of its body through mitosis. Many simple one-celled organisms, like yeast or bacteria, can use this process of cell division to produce new organisms through

_____asexual reproduction_____, in which a single parent produces offspring through mitosis. Most organisms, however, are reproduced from two parents in a process

called _____sexual reproduction_____. In this process cells from two parents combine

to form a _____zygote_____, which contains genetic material from each parent. Organisms produce reproductive cells through a process called

_____meiosis_____, which reduces the number of chromosomes in the reproductive cells, so they don't end up with twice as many as they need.

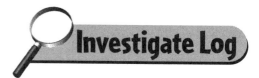
# The Stages of a Mealworm's Life

## Materials

mealworm culture

paper plate

hand lens

## Activity Procedure

**1** Your teacher will give you a mealworm from the mealworm culture.

**2** Put the mealworm on the paper plate. Using the hand lens, **observe** the mealworm closely. Draw what you see.

**3** Label these parts on your drawing: head, segment, antenna, outer shell, claw, mouth, and leg.

**4** **Observe** the mealworm's movements. Does it move straight forward or from side to side? Does it move quickly or slowly? **Record** your observations.

**5** Now your teacher will give you a beetle from the mealworm culture. Repeat Steps 2–4 with the beetle.

**6** Finally, **observe** the mealworm culture. Try to find evidence of other stages of a mealworm's life, such as eggs and pupa cases. Draw pictures of what you find.

**7** **Compare** your drawings of the eggs and pupa cases with your drawings of the mealworm and the beetle. Form a **hypothesis** about the order of these life stages. Then list the ways in which a mealworm changes as it grows.

Name _____

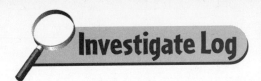

## Draw Conclusions

1. How are the mealworm and the beetle similar? Possible answers: Both have
heads and antennae, both have segmented bodies, and both have legs.

_____

2. How is the beetle different from the mealworm? Possible answers: The
beetle has a hard shell and wings, and the mealworm doesn't; the beetle has
more legs.

_____

3. **Scientists at Work** Scientists often **observe** an organism and then **hypothesize**
about their observations. What observations enabled you to form your
hypothesis about the order of the life stages? Accept all reasonable answers.

_____

_____

**Investigate Further** **Plan and conduct a simple investigation** to test your
hypothesis about the life stages of a mealworm. Decide what equipment or
technology you will need to use to test your hypothesis. Then use the equipment
or technology in your investigation. _____

_____

_____

# Hypothesize

To explain your observations you may form a hypothesis. A hypothesis is an explanation that you can test. Tests cannot prove a hypothesis. They can only support it. If test results don't support your hypothesis, then you need to form a new one.

## Think About Hypothesizing

People used to believe that certain forms of life developed directly from nonliving things, such as dead animals or mud. This was known as spontaneous generation. The belief was a hypothesis based on observation. Eventually the hypothesis was subjected to scientific testing and found to be incorrect. See if you can think of ways to test the following hypotheses.

1. Many years ago maggots were believed to come from decaying meat. Suppose you are living in those days and you propose a new hypothesis that maggots hatch from fly eggs laid on the meat. How can you test your hypothesis?

   _____

   _____

   _____

   _____

2. Microorganisms were believed to arise spontaneously in water under certain conditions. For example, if you add hay to water and wait a few days, you will be able to use a microscope and find microorganisms in the water. What hypothesis could you form about this observation? How could you test it?

   _____

   _____

   _____

3. In 1745 an Englishman named John Needham wanted to show that microorganisms spring spontaneously from meat broth. It was known that boiling would kill any microorganisms in the broth. His hypothesis was that if microorganisms appeared in broth that had been boiled, then spontaneous generation would be proved. Do you agree with his hypothesis? Why or why not?

   _____

   _____

Name _____

Date _____

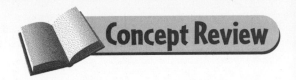
# What Is a Life Cycle?

## Lesson Concept

A life cycle is made of the stages that make up an organism's life. Some organisms grow through direct development, in which the only change is size. Others go through metamorphosis, which means they change shape and characteristics as they grow.

## Vocabulary

**life cycle** (A46)    **direct development** (A46)    **metamorphosis** (A47)

Match the term on the left with the sentence on the right that describes it by writing the letter of the description in the blank next to the term.

### Column A

___E___ **1.** molting

___F___ **2.** metamorphosis

___G___ **3.** larva

___H___ **4.** life cycle

___D___ **5.** complete metamorphosis

___C___ **6.** pupa

___B___ **7.** adult

___A___ **8.** cocoon

### Column B

**A** A pupa may bury itself in the ground or it may make a protective covering around itself.

**B** When an organism reaches its final stage of development, it is able to reproduce.

**C** During the third stage of complete metamorphosis, insects neither eat nor move.

**D** Some insects have a life cycle that includes four distinct stages.

**E** Some insects that go through incomplete metamorphosis must shed their outer skeletons as they grow.

**F** Some organisms go through drastic changes in the shape or characteristics of their bodies.

**G** In complete metamorphosis, when an insect hatches from its egg, it enters the second stage of its development.

**H** Most organisms grow and mature through several distinct stages of life.

Name _____

Date _____

# Inherited Characteristics

## Materials

mirror

## Activity Procedure

**1** Use the chart below for this activity.

**2** **Tongue Rolling** Use the mirror to **observe** what you are doing. Stick out your tongue, and try to roll its edges up toward the center. **Record** your results in the chart.

**3** **Ear Lobes** Use the mirror to **observe** the shape of your ear lobes. Are they attached to your cheek, or do they hang free? **Record** your results in the chart.

| Characteristic | Results (Circle one) | | Class Totals |
|---|---|---|---|
| Tongue rolling | Yes | No | |
| Ear lobes | Attached | Free | |
| Folded hands | Left | Right | |

**4** **Folded Hands** Clasp your hands in front of you. **Observe** which of your thumbs falls naturally on top. **Record** your results in the chart.

**5** Your teacher will now ask students to report the results of their observations. Tally the results in the chart as students report them. Total the number of students for each characteristic. Then **calculate** what fraction of the class has each characteristic.

Name _____

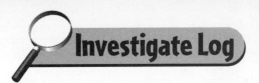

## Draw Conclusions

**1. Infer** whether a person could learn tongue rolling. Explain. If tongue rolling is
inherited, a person could not learn to roll his or her tongue.

_____

**2.** What other inherited characteristics could you have **observed?**
Possible answers include eye color, hair color, left- or right-handedness,
and freckles.

_____

_____

**3. Scientists at Work** Scientists often **use numbers** to summarize the data they
collect. Which trait in each pair occurred most often in your class?
Answers will vary.

_____

_____

**Investigate Further** Do your class results suggest how often these traits occur in
other people? Choose one or two of these characteristics. **Predict** whether the
results will be the same for another group. Then ask some of your friends,
neighbors, and family members to participate in this activity, and **observe** the

results. **Record** the results, and share them with your class. _____

_____

_____

# Use Numbers

When you use numbers, you summarize the data you collect. You can also use numbers to estimate, to count, and to figure out ratios or percentages.

## Think About Using Numbers

Greg was experimenting with cross-breeding pea plants. He started with 100 plants. One of the things he wanted to study was seed color. When Greg crossed 50 plants having yellow seeds with 50 plants having green seeds, all the offspring had yellow seeds.

**1.** What percentage of this first generation had yellow seeds? _____

**2.** Greg knew there would be two factors for seed color in each plant and that the factors would pair up. He represented this first generation with the following chart, using Y for what he began calling the yellow seed factor and G for the green seed factor.

|   | **G** | **G** |
|---|---|---|
| **Y** | YG | YG |
| **Y** | YG | YG |

The parents with green seeds were GG and the parents with yellow seeds were YY. Looking at his chart, he realized that even though every offspring's seed was yellow, each offspring's seed also carried a factor for green.

**3.** Next Greg planted all the yellow seeds from the offspring. When the plants grew up, he checked their seeds and found that 75 percent of them were yellow. The rest were green seeds. What percentage of this second generation of

pea plants had green seeds? _____

**4.** Greg represented this second generation with another chart. This time he knew that each parent plant had factors of both Y and G. Each square in the chart represents one-fourth the total number of seeds. What percent is represented by GG?

|   | **Y** | **G** |
|---|---|---|
| **Y** | YY | YG |
| **G** | YG | GG |

_____

**5.** What percent of the total number of seeds carried at least one Y factor?

_____

**Use with page A51.**

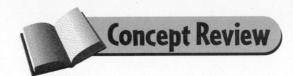
# Why Are Offspring Like Their Parents?

## Lesson Concept

Many traits are inherited by offspring from their parents. These traits are determined genes. Gene combinations determine if traits are seen (dominant traits) or hidden (recessive traits).

## Vocabulary

**inherited trait** (A52)                    **dominant trait** (A53)

**recessive trait** (A53)                    **gene** (A54)

Look at the traits shown for two generations in this family. Label the traits *D* for "dominant," *R* for "recessive," or *N* for "not inherited."

### First Generation

**Dad**
Free earlobes
Short eyelashes
Plays tennis
Speaks English and French

**Mom**
Attached earlobes
Long eyelashes
Grows tomatoes
Speaks Spanish and English

### Second Generation

| **Son** | **Daughter** | **Daughter** | **Son** |
|---|---|---|---|
| Free earlobes _D_ | Free earlobes _D_ | Attached earlobes _R_ | Free earlobes _D_ |
| Plays basketball _N_ | Grows tomatoes _N_ | Plays basketball _N_ | Plays tennis and basketball _N_ |
| Speaks Spanish and English _N_ | Speaks Spanish, French, and English _N_ | Speaks only English _N_ | Speaks Spanish and English _N_ |
| Short eyelashes _R_ | Long eyelashes _D_ | Long eyelashes _D_ | Long eyelashes _D_ |

Name _____

Date _____

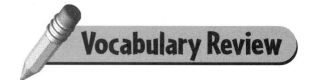 

# Recognize Vocabulary

**Underline the vocabulary term that best completes each sentence.**

1. Gametes, or reproductive cells, are formed during        .
   **A** meiosis      **B** mitosis      **C** metamorphosis    **D** asexual reproduction

2. The DNA codes for a certain trait are found on a        .
   **A** inherited trait    **B** dominant trait    **C** recessive trait    **D** gene

3. The code that tells each cell when to divide is contained in a threadlike        .
   **A** gene      **B** life cycle      **C** mitosis      **D** chromosome

4. Worms change only in size as they grow to be adults, because they go through ___.
   **A** direct development    **B** mitosis    **C** metamorphosis    **D** asexual reproduction

5. When two parents each contribute a cell to form one cell, that's        .
   **A** asexual reproduction    **B** sexual reproduction    **C** meiosis    **D** gene

6. Development and growth in an egg is the first stage of a bird's        .
   **A** metamorphosis    **B** direct development    **C** life cycle    **D** asexual reproduction

7. Hair color is an example of a(n)        .
   **A** inherited trait    **B** dominant trait    **C** recessive trait    **D** gene

8. The transformation of a caterpillar to a butterfly is an example of        .
   **A** direct development    **B** mitosis    **C** metamorphosis    **D** asexual reproduction

9. If you scrape your skin, your body creates new skin cells through        .
   **A** meiosis    **B** mitosis    **C** metamorphosis    **D** sexual reproduction

10. Yeast, a one-celled organism, reproduces by budding, a type of        .
    **A** asexual reproduction    **B** sexual reproduction    **C** meiosis    **D** gene

11. Gregor Mendel found that in peas, tallness was a strong, or        .
    **A** inherited trait    **B** dominant trait    **C** recessive trait    **D** gene

# Chapter 3 • Graphic Organizer for Chapter Concepts

## Types of Plants and Their Adaptations

# The Parts of a Plant

## Materials

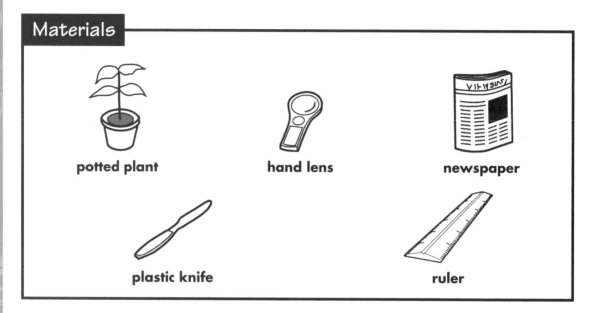

potted plant     hand lens     newspaper

plastic knife     ruler

## Activity Procedure

1. Make a drawing of the plant. List all the parts of the plant that you can name.

2. **Observe** the leaves. What colors are they? Use the ruler to measure the length and width of the leaves. Are they all the same shape and size? Are they wide or narrow? Are they long or short? Do they grow singly or in pairs? Observe them more closely with the hand lens. What more can you say about them? Identify and label the leaves in your drawing.

3. **Observe** the stem. Does it bend? Does it have branches? What more can you say about it? Identify and label the stem in your drawing.

4. Hold the pot upside down over the newspaper. Tap the pot gently until the plant and the soil come out. If the plant won't come out, run the plastic knife around between the soil and the inside of the pot.

5. Shake the soil from the roots until you can see them clearly. **Observe** the roots. Is there a single root, or are there many small roots? What shape are the roots? Use the ruler to **measure** the length of the roots. Are they thick or thin? Long or short? Use the hand lens to observe them more closely. What more can you say about them? Identify and label the roots in your drawing.

6. Put the soil and the plant back into the pot. Water the plant lightly to help it recover from being out of the pot.

Name _____

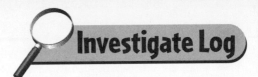
**Investigate Log**

## Draw Conclusions

**1.** What are the parts of the plant you **observed**? leaves, stem, roots

_____

**2.** **Compare** the plant parts you identified with the parts of a large tree. How are they the same? How are they different? Possible answers: A tree's stem, or trunk, is harder, taller, and larger than a potted plant's stem; the leaves are similar; the tree leaves are larger; the roots of a tree are larger and hard like the trunk.

_____

**3.** **Scientists at Work** Scientists learn by making observations. What did you **observe** about each part of the plant? Answers could include: veins or tiny hairs on the leaves, different leaf shapes, branched stems, flexible stems, branched roots, root hairs, and different colors and shapes of leaves.

_____

**Investigate Further** **Observe** a different type of plant. Then identify its parts. Does it have the same parts as the plant you observed in the activity? Do the parts look the same as the parts you observed in the activity? All plants have the same main parts. The parts of some plants may look different. For example, leaves may have different shapes.

_____

# Observe

Observing involves using one or more of the senses to perceive properties of objects or events. Sometimes you need to use an instrument, such as a microscope, to extend your senses.

### Think About Observing

Suppose you are walking beside a river on a summer afternoon. You observe several large slabs of concrete on the riverbank. When you look across the river, you observe more concrete slabs on the opposite bank. You are curious about them, but you decide to move on. After a short while, you come to a pipe that empties into the river. The water is foamy and cloudy near the pipe. It has no smell. You observe a lot of plants growing in the cloudy water and on the riverbank near the pipe.

1. What objects have you observed on your walk? _____

_____

2. What senses have you used? _____

3. You observed something coming from the pipe. From your observations, do you think it was harmful to the plants? _____

_____

_____

4. How could you make a better observation about what was coming from the pipe? _____

5. If you decided to observe the foam more closely, what do you think you should be looking for? _____

_____

6. If you decided to observe the concrete slabs more closely, would you need instruments to extend your senses? _____

_____

Name _____

Date _____

# What Are the Functions of Roots, Stems, and Leaves?

## Lesson Concept

Each part of a plant has a different function. Roots anchor the plant and take in minerals and water. A stem supports the plant and moves materials between its parts. Leaves make food.

## Vocabulary

**xylem** (A69)          **phloem** (A69)          **chlorophyll** (A70)

Match each term on the left with its description on the right.

**Column A**

_____ **1.** fibrous roots

_____ **2.** phloem

_____ **3.** stomata

_____ **4.** chlorophyll

_____ **5.** xylem

_____ **6.** taproot

_____ **7.** stem

_____ **8.** leaf

_____ **9.** root hairs

_____ **10.** chloroplasts

_____ **11.** prop roots

**Column B**

**A** tiny holes in a leaf where carbon dioxide enters and oxygen exits

**B** a pigment that helps plants use light energy to make sugars

**C** a plant part that holds the plant up and carries food and water to other plant parts

**D** tiny parts of roots that take in water and minerals from the soil

**E** a root that goes straight down so it can reach water deep underground

**F** a plant part that is the "food factory" of the plant

**G** roots that form a thick and tangled mat just under the surface of the soil

**H** the parts in leaf cells where the food-making process takes place

**I** tubes in plant stems that carry water and minerals

**J** tubes in plant stems that carry food made in the leaves to other parts of the plant

**K** roots that begin above ground so they can keep trees growing in loose, wet soil from being blown over by the wind

# Simple Plants

## Materials

moss                    liverwort                    hand lens

## Activity Procedure

**1** **Observe** the moss and the liverwort. **Record** what you see.

**2** Now **observe** the plants with a hand lens. Can you see different parts? Do any of the parts you see look like the parts of the potted plant you observed in Lesson 1?

**3** **Observe** the plants by touching them with your fingers. Are they soft or firm? Are they dry or moist? What else can you tell by feeling them? Describe what they feel like.

**4** Touch the plants with a pencil or other object while you **observe** them through the hand lens. Do the parts bend, or are they stiff? Do you see anything new if you push a part of the plant to one side? Describe what you see.

**5** **Observe** the plants by smelling them. Do they have any kind of odor? Try to identify the odors. Describe what you smell.

**6** Make drawings of the moss and liverwort, identify the parts you observed, and **infer** what each part does.

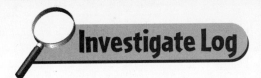
## Draw Conclusions

1. What plant parts did you **observe** on the moss? What parts did you observe on the liverwort? Students should observe stemlike, leaflike, and rootlike structures on both plants.

2. What do you **infer** each part of the plant does? Students may infer that the leaflike structures make food, the stemlike structures hold the leaves, and the rootlike structures anchor the plants and absorb water.

3. **Scientists at Work** Scientists use observations to **compare** things. Use the observations you made in this investigation to compare the moss and liverwort with the plant you observed in Lesson 1. The parts of the moss and liverwort seem similar to the parts of the potted plant.

**Investigate Further** Observe a fern. How does it **compare** with the moss and the liverwort? The fern's parts look more like the roots, the stems, and the leaves of the potted plant than do the parts of the moss and the liverwort.

# Compare

When you compare, you observe objects or events and try to find out how they are alike or different. You ask yourself questions while you are observing. Which plant is the smallest? Which plant has the most leaves? What does this plant have that the other does not have?

## Think About Comparing

When you shop for fruits and vegetables, you see all different shapes and colors. You know from your experience that each of the items also has its own special taste and smell. All the shapes, the colors, the tastes, and the smells come from plants. Answer the questions about the following items: watermelon, cantaloupe, strawberries, carrots, apples, mushrooms, and lettuce.

1. Compare the mushrooms to the strawberries. Do they share any

    characteristics? How are they different? _____

    _____

    _____

    _____

    _____

2. How is the carrot different from all the other items? _____

3. Compare the lettuce to all the other items. Can you think of an important

    difference? _____

    _____

    _____

    _____

    _____

4. Choose the two items you think are most similar to one another. Explain your

    choice. _____

    _____

5. Choose the two items you think are most different from one another. Explain

    your choice. _____

    _____

Name _____

Date _____

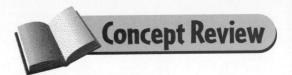 

# What Are the Two Major Groups of Plants?

## Lesson Concept

Vascular plants have xylem and phloem. Nonvascular plants do not have these tubes. Nonvascular plants and simple vascular plants reproduce with spores. Gymnosperms and angiosperms are seed-producing vascular plants. Plants go through several stages in their life cycles.

## Vocabulary

| | | |
|---|---|---|
| **nonvascular** (A74) | **vascular** (A74) | **spore** (A75) |
| **gymnosperm** (A76) | **pollen** (A76) | **angiosperm** (A77) |

Put each term on the list following into the Venn diagram below. Remember, in a Venn diagram, the areas where circles overlap are areas that include both categories shown in the circles. If a term belongs in or applies to both categories, put it in the area where the circles overlap. If it belongs in or applies to only one category, put it into the correct circle.

| | | | |
|---|---|---|---|
| **spore** | **conifer** | **pollen** | **flower** |
| **fruit** | **mosses** | **ferns** | **apples** |
| **xylem** | **phloem** | **chloroplasts** | **life cycle** |

# Popcorn

## Materials

large plastic measuring cup  balance  unpopped popcorn

## Activity Procedure

1. Cover the bottom of the measuring cup with unpopped popcorn seeds.

2. **Estimate** the volume of the unpopped seeds. Put the cup on the balance, and **measure** the mass of the unpopped seeds.

3. **Predict** what will happen to the mass and the volume when the seeds are popped.

4. Your teacher will help you pop the popcorn. Return the popped seeds to the measuring cup.

5. **Measure** the volume and mass of the cup of popped popcorn. Were your **predictions** correct?

Name _____

## Draw Conclusions

**1.** How did the volume of the popcorn change? The volume increased.

_____

**2.** How did the mass change? Explain. The mass of the popped popcorn should be slightly less, because the water escaped as steam during popping.

_____

**3. Scientists at Work** One reason why scientists **experiment** is to test predictions. If an experiment doesn't turn out the way they predicted, it may mean that their predictions were wrong. Or it may mean that they did not consider everything that could affect the experiment. Did you predict the volume and mass of the popped popcorn correctly? Explain.

Possible answer: No; failure to predict the mass correctly was probably due to forgetting about the water that was lost from the seeds as steam.

_____

**Investigate Further** Water turns into a gas when it is heated. What do you **predict** will happen when that gas cools? **Experiment** to test your prediction.

_____

_____

_____

# Experiment

When you experiment, you gather data to test a hypothesis. A well-designed experiment will allow you to test for certain variables while controlling others so you will know which factors affect the outcome.

## Think About Experimenting

Juan and Ahmal were planning an experiment to see which of four different fertilizers would grow the biggest and healthiest plants. Juan gathered four pots from the garage, labeled them *Pot A* through *Pot D*, and filled them with dirt from his backyard. He put various seeds into each pot. He labeled the fertilizers *A* through *D* and put a teaspoon of *Fertilizer A* into *Pot A*, *Fertilizer B* in *Pot B*, and so on until each pot had a spoonful of different fertilizer. Ahmal watched him do this. Then he reminded Juan that he had not controlled his experiment. Juan agreed. They started over again.

1. What are some variables Juan should control? _____

_____

_____

2. Juan and Ahmal also need a control sample. How do they make one?

_____

_____

3. As he was filling the pots with potting soil he had bought at the hardware store, Juan thought of another problem. What if, without meaning to, they paid more attention to one of the plants, because they had already formed a hypothesis that *Fertilizer A* worked better than the others? How could they avoid this? _____

_____

_____

4. What do you think would be the best way to gather data from this experiment?

_____

_____

# How Do People Use Plants?

## Lesson Concept

People eat the leaves, the stems, the roots, the seeds, the fruits, and the flowers of various plants. When they are sick, people often use medicines made from plants. In fact, many things people use every day come from plants.

## Vocabulary

| grain (A82) | fiber (A84) |
|---|---|

**Read the statements below. Put a _T_ in front of the true statements and an _F_ in front of the false statements. If the statement is false, write a correction in the space provided after it.**

_____T_____ **1.** People use plants more for food than for any other purpose.

_____

_____

_____F_____ **2.** Fruits form the largest part of the Food Guide Pyramid.
Grains form the largest part of the Food Guide Pyramid.

_____

_____F_____ **3.** Quinine, which is made from the bark of a tree, is used to treat measles. Quinine is used to treat malaria.

_____

_____T_____ **4.** Grains are the seeds of certain types of grasses. _____

_____

_____F_____ **5.** Digitalis, which is made from the leaves of the maple tree, is a heart medicine. Digitalis is made from the leaves of the foxglove plant.

_____

_____T_____ **6.** A fiber is any material that can be separated into thread.

_____

_____

Name _____

Date _____

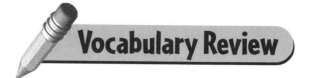 

# Recognize Vocabulary

Read the clues to decide which vocabulary term to use to fill in the word puzzle.

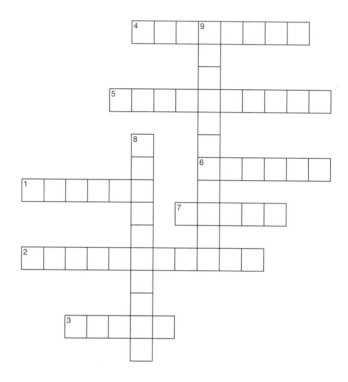

## Across

1. tubes that carry food in plants
2. plants that lack tubes for carrying food and water
3. a reproductive cell that grows into a new plant
4. plants that have tubes for carrying food and water
5. a plant with seeds covered by fruit
6. plant structures that contain male reproductive cells
7. tubes that carry water and minerals in plants

## Down

8. a plant whose seeds are not protected by fruit
9. a pigment that helps plants produce sugar from light energy

# Chapter 4 • Graphic Organizer for Chapter Concepts

## Plant Processes

# How Plants Use Leaves

## Materials

3 potted plants          labels          scissors

meterstick          measuring cup

## Activity Procedure

**1** Label the plants *Normal*, *Half*, and *None*.

**2** Using scissors, carefully cut off all the leaves of the plant labeled *None*. Cut off half the leaves of the plant labeled *Half*. The number of leaves is the variable.

**3** Don't do anything to the plant labeled *Normal*. This plant is the control.

**4** Use the meterstick to **measure** the height of each plant. **Record** the heights.

**5** Put all three plants in a place where they will get plenty of sunlight. Water the plants as needed. Use the measuring cup to ensure they all get the same amount of water. What do you **hypothesize** about how the plants will grow?

**6** **Measure** the heights of the plants every day, and **record** your data. Record anything else you **observe** about the plants. Cut off any new leaves that grow on the plants labeled *Half* and *None*.

**7** At the end of two weeks, review your data.

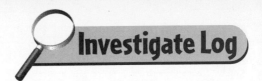

**Investigate Log**

## Draw Conclusions

**1.** Which plant grew the most in height? Which plant grew the least? Does the data support your **hypothesis**? What can you conclude about the importance of leaves? Answers may vary, but the most growth should be in the plant labeled *Normal*, and the least growth in the plant labeled *None*. Leaves are very important in plant growth.

**2.** Why was making sure the three plants received the same amount of sunlight important in this investigation? You are trying to find out what effect cutting off leaves will have on growth. If everything else is not the same for the three plants, you can't be sure what caused any changes you observed.

**3.** **Scientists at Work** Scientists always **control variables** when they **experiment**. Why was watering all the plants with the same amount of water important in your investigation? To be certain that a second variable, amount of water, would not alter the results of the experiment.

**Investigate Further** Does adding plant food really improve plant growth, as advertisements would have you believe? **Plan and conduct a simple investigation** to find out. Be sure you have a way to **control variables** in your investigation.

_____

_____

_____

_____

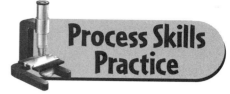

# Control Variables

When you control variables, you are better able to draw valid conclusions about the data you collect in an experiment. The first step is to identify which conditions in an experiment may change the experiment's outcome. Then you control all but one of those conditions.

## Think About Controlling Variables

Mary has a large pond stocked with several kinds of fish. She has been feeding the fish the same food for years, and her fish have always been healthy. Now she has found another brand of food that is less expensive. She is concerned, however, that the new brand will not be as good for her fish as the more expensive brand. To experiment, she takes water from the pond and puts the same amount into two identical aquarium tanks. She puts a few fish in each tank, making sure that each tank has the same number, kind, and size of fish. She sprinkles the old brand of fish food in one tank and the new brand in the other tank. After one week Mary sees that the fish in both tanks are still healthy. After another week all the fish are still healthy, but some of the fish eating the new brand of food have actually grown larger.

1. What are the variables in Mary's experiment? _____

   _____

   _____

   _____

2. Which of the variables did Mary deliberately change? _____

3. Mary forgot to control one other important variable. Which one was it?

   _____

4. How do you think having two uncontrolled variables will affect the

   experiment? _____

   _____

5. Other than the type of food, can you think of another variable that may

   explain why the fish got bigger in one tank? _____

   _____

   _____

   _____

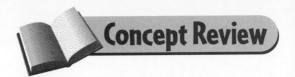

# How Do Plants Make Food?

## Lesson Concept

Plants make food in their leaves by photosynthesis, the process in which chlorophyll uses light energy to combine water and carbon dioxide to form glucose and oxygen. Plants use most of this food and store the rest. The extra food is passed to animals that eat the plants. Plants and animals use food energy, which is released by cellular respiration.

## Vocabulary

**photosynthesis** (A96)          **epidermis** (A97)          **palisade layer** (A97)

**cellular respiration** (A100)

Match each term on the left with its description on the right.

### Column A

____J____ **1.** upper epidermis

____F____ **2.** glucose

____I____ **3.** cellular respiration

____H____ **4.** palisade layer

____A____ **5.** photosynthesis

____K____ **6.** guard cells

____B____ **7.** chlorophyll

____E____ **8.** chloroplasts

____D____ **9.** spongy layer

____G____ **10.** cuticle

____C____ **11.** veins

### Column B

**A** a process by which plants make food

**B** a substance in chloroplasts that changes light energy into chemical energy

**C** the system of xylem and phloem tubes in leaves

**D** a layer of cells that lies below the palisade layer and has many air spaces

**E** structures that contain chlorophyll, which gives plants their green color

**F** a type of sugar made in leaves

**G** the waxy covering of the epidermis

**H** a layer of cells that have many chloroplasts and that lie directly below the upper epidermis

**I** a process by which plants release the energy in food to carry on life processes

**J** the single layer of protective cells on the upper surface of a leaf

**K** cells that form the edges of the stomata

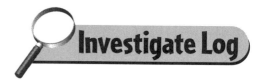

# How Plants Get the Light They Need

## Materials

3 labels     2 potted plants     measuring cup     water

## Activity Procedure

1. Write *Odd days* on one of the labels. Put the label on one side of a pot. Write *Even days* on a second label. Put this label on the other side of the same pot. Write *Don't move* on the third label, and put it on the other pot.

2. Place both potted plants in a sunny area. If you don't have a sunny area, put them under and to one side of a light source, such as a lamp. Make sure both plants are on the same side of and at the same distance from the lamp.

3. Use the measuring cup to give both plants the same amount of water at the same time each day. **Observe** the plants every day, and **record** your observations.

4. Turn the plant labeled *Odd days/Even days* one-half turn every day. If you start the **experiment** on an even-numbered day, place the pot so you can see the *Even days* label. If you start on an odd-numbered day, place the pot so that you can see the *Odd days* label. Do not turn the plant labeled *Don't move*.

5. After ten days write a summary of your **observations** about how the plants have grown. Draw pictures showing how the plants looked at the beginning and at the end of the **experiment**.

Name _____

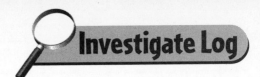

## Draw Conclusions

**1.** What did you **observe** about the growth of the plants during the investigation?

One plant grew toward the light, and the other plant did not.

**2. Compare** the two plants. What variable were the plants responding to?

the side facing the light

**3. Scientists at Work** Scientists often **compare** organisms to help them understand how organisms respond to their environments. In this investigation, how did comparing the way the plants grew help you

**draw conclusions** about the way plants respond to light? Answers should

include the idea that comparing the plants helped students understand that

plants will grow toward the light they need for survival.

**Investigate Further Hypothesize** about all plants needing the same amount of sunlight. Try putting two different plants in a very sunny window. Give both plants the same amount of water. **Observe**, and **record** your observations

of the plants for two weeks. _____

_____

_____

# Draw Conclusions

When you draw conclusions, you use many other process skills, such as processing data collected from literature research.

## Think About Drawing Conclusions

Jason was buying grass seed for his mother's lawn. His mother wanted the grass to grow well under the maple trees, in the direct sun at the south side of the house, and in the moist shaded area at the bottom of the backyard slope. Jason went to the garden center and looked at the different types of grass seed. Each bag of seed had a description of what the grass would look like and where it would grow best. He took the following notes:

Jackson Brand: dark green, thick "carpet," grows well in shade, keep out of full sun, turns green in mid-March, goes dormant (brown) at first frost

Black Beard Grass: dark green, average thickness, grows best in moist, shaded areas, stays green all year

Wicked Weed Grass: medium green, medium thickness, needs full sun, turns green in mid-March, goes dormant at first frost

**1.** Fill in the chart to help in drawing conclusions.

|  | **Jackson Brand** | **Black Beard** | **Wicked Weed** |
|---|---|---|---|
| Color |  |  |  |
| Thickness |  |  |  |
| Needs sun or shade |  |  |  |
| When it turns green |  |  |  |
| When it goes dormant |  |  |  |

**2.** What conclusions can you draw from the data in the chart? _____

_____

_____

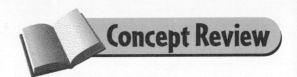
Concept Review

# How Do Plants Respond to Light and Gravity?

## Lesson Concept

Tropisms cause plants to respond to certain stimuli, such as light and gravity. Some plants respond to touch.

## Vocabulary

**tropism** (A104)     **phototropism** (A104)     **gravitropism** (A105)

Write a *T* in front of the true statements and an *F* in front of the false statements. If the statement is false, write a correction to it in the space provided.

_____ **1.** A plant's response to a stimulus is called a tropism. _____

_____

_____ **2.** Gravitropism is an adaptation that causes some plants to live longer than others. Gravitropism is an adaptation that makes sure a plant's roots grow down into the soil and that the stems grow upward.

_____ **3.** Some plants have parts that can move in response to being touched.

_____

_____ **4.** If a seed lands upside down, its roots will grow upward and may never touch the soil. Gravitropism will cause the roots to respond to the pull of gravity and grow toward the soil.

_____ **5.** Phototropism is a plant's response to light. _____

_____ **6.** A stimulus is anything that causes an organism to respond.

_____

_____ **7.** A plant bends toward the light, because the cells on the side of the plant facing the light are shorter. _____

_____

# Flower Parts

### Materials

| fresh flower | paper towel | hand lens | ruler |

### Activity Procedure

1. Place a fresh flower on a paper towel.

2. **Observe** the outside of the flower. Notice the green, leaflike parts around the petals. These are called *sepals* (SEE•puhls). How many sepals does the flower have? What shape are the sepals? **Record** your observations.

3. Now **observe** the flower's petals. How many petals does the flower have? What shape are they? What color are they? Do the petals have any patterns, or are they one color? What do the petals feel like? **Record** your observations.

4. **Observe** the flower with your eyes closed. Does it have an odor? How would you describe the odor? What part of the flower do you think the odor is coming from? **Record** your observations about the flower's odor.

5. Using the hand lens, **observe** the inside of the flower. What parts do you see? What are the shapes of these parts? **Measure** these parts. **Record** your observations about the inside of the flower.

6. Now make a drawing of the inside of the flower. As you draw each part, try to **infer** what it does.

Name _____

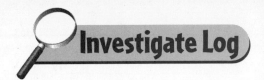 Investigate Log

## Draw Conclusions

**1.** Colorful markings and strong odors often attract birds and insects to flowers. How might the location of the markings and odors attract birds and insects to the flower? The colorful markings are on the petals that surround the inner parts of the flower. The strong odors seem to come from the inner structures themselves.

**2.** In the very center of a flower is the female reproductive part. Stalks surrounding the center contain male reproductive parts. **Infer** how it might help the plant to have the male parts around the female part. Answers will vary; students might infer that pollen could fall or blow from the male parts onto the female part or that insects touching the male parts could transfer pollen to the female part.

**3. Scientists at Work** When scientists **infer** a part's function, they sometimes base their inferences on **observing** the part's location. Based on the sepals' location, what could you infer about the function of sepals? They protect the delicate petals and inner parts of a flower.

**Investigate Further** **Observe** the parts of another kind of flower. How does that flower **compare** to the one you observed in this investigation? Does it have the same number of sepals? Are the petals arranged the same way? Do the flower's inner parts look the same? What other questions could you answer by observing the flower? _____

Name _____

Date _____

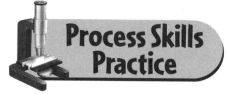

# Infer

When you infer, you explain an event by using observation, previous information or experience, and your own judgment. Inferences supported by observation and reasoning are always valid, but they may not always be correct.

## Think About Inferring

Tami saw an article in the newspaper about the poor apple harvest in her area. Farmers were blaming the poor harvest on the heavy rains that had fallen earlier that year. One farmer interviewed for the article said, "There was so much rain in the spring that the bees couldn't get out. Those that did go out of their hives were knocked to the ground and drowned." Tami was confused. She asked herself, "What do bees have to do with a poor apple harvest?"

1. What event was Tami trying to explain? _____

2. What observations can she use? _____
   _____

3. What previous knowledge or experience could Tami use to help her
   understand why the apple harvest was poor? _____
   _____
   _____

4. Tami tries an inference: perhaps the bees add honey to the apples to make them
   sweeter. What are some reasons this inference might be wrong? _____
   _____
   _____

5. Can you think of one inference Tami could make based on her observations
   that would be valid? _____
   _____

**Use with page A109.**

Name _____

Date _____

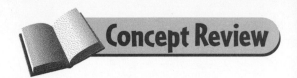
Concept Review

# How Do Plants Reproduce?

## Lesson Concept

Most flowers have both male and female reproductive parts. Pollen, which has sperm cells, is produced by the stamens. The pistil has the eggs. Pollen is transferred from the stamens to the pistil. After fertilization, the eggs develop into seeds.

## Vocabulary

**fertilization** (A110)      **stamens** (A110)      **pistil** (A110)      **ovary** (A111)

**Answer each of the questions below by writing *yes* or *no* in the space on the left. Then, on the lines beneath the question, explain your answer.**

___no___ **1.** Do most flowers have only female reproductive parts? Most flowers have both male and female reproductive parts.

___no___ **2.** Do the stamens have eggs? Stamens produce pollen, which contains sperm.

___no___ **3.** Is pollen transferred from the pistil to the stamens? Pollen is produced in the stamens and is transferred to the pistil.

___yes___ **4.** Is the pistil the flower's female reproductive part? The pistil contains the flower's female reproductive cells.

___no___ **5.** Do animals carry eggs from one flower to another? Animals carry pollen from one flower to another.

___yes___ **6.** Do some plants depend on the wind to transfer pollen? Wind carries pollen from some plants to others.

___no___ **7.** Do gymnosperms have flowers? Gymnosperms are cone-bearing plants that do not have flowers.

___no___ **8.** Are fertilization and pollination the same thing? Pollination is the transfer of pollen from a male part to a female part. Fertilization is the joining of male and female reproductive cells.

# The Parts of a Seed

## Materials

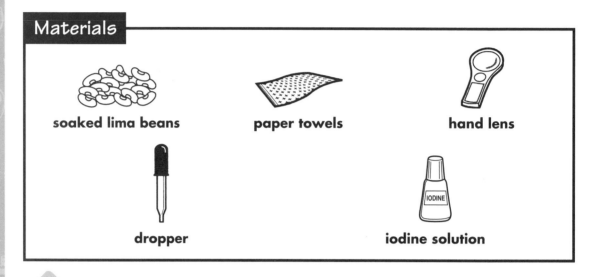

soaked lima beans      paper towels      hand lens

dropper      iodine solution

**CAUTION** **Activity Procedure**

**1** Put a soaked lima bean on a paper towel. **Observe** the seed with the hand lens. **Record** your observations by drawing a picture of what you see.

**2** Carefully peel away the outer covering of the bean. This covering is called the *seed coat*.

**3** Gently open the bean by splitting it in half. Use the hand lens to **observe** the parts inside the bean. **Record** your observations by drawing a picture of what you see.

**4** Using the point of a pencil, carefully remove the part of the bean that looks like a tiny plant. This is called the *embryo*. Look through the hand lens to identify the parts of the embryo that look like leaves, a stem, and a root.

**5** **CAUTION** **Iodine can stain your hands and clothes**. Carefully, put a drop or two of the iodine solution on the other parts of the bean. These parts are called the *cotyledons*. **Observe** what happens. **Record** your observations.

**6** Label the seed coat, embryo, and cotyledons on your drawing from Step 3. On the embryo, label the parts that look like leaves, a stem, and a root.

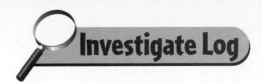

**Investigate Log**

## Draw Conclusions

**1.** What words would you use to describe the seed coat of the bean? What do you **infer** is its function? Answers may vary; words may include *hard* and *tough.* Students should infer that it has a protective function.

_____

**2.** Iodine turns black in the presence of starch, a kind of food that plants store. Because of this, what do you **infer** is the function of the cotyledons? to provide food for the embryo as it grows

_____

**3. Scientists at Work** Scientists **observe** many plant parts. They often **communicate** to other scientists inferences they have made about the functions of certain parts. They use descriptions, data tables, graphs, and drawings. How would you communicate to a classmate your inferences about the function of cotyledons? Possible answer: with a description of the results of dropping iodine onto the cotyledons. Since the cotyledons turn black, they must contain starch. The embryo could use the starch as food as it grows..

**Investigate Further** **Observe** other seeds that can be easily opened, such as green peas, squash seeds, or watermelon seeds. Examine the seed coats, and then gently split the seeds open. **Compare** them to the bean seed you studied in this investigation. Draw pictures, and label the parts of the seeds you observe.

_____

_____

_____

# Communicate

When you communicate, you give information. In science you communicate by showing results from an activity in an organized way, such as by using a chart. Then you and other people can interpret the results.

## Think About Communicating

Richard was working in his basement laboratory every night. He was trying to invent a new kind of glue that would stick to almost everything but would not be poisonous. He decided to use only things that you can eat. He mixed flour with water. It was a good glue, but Richard was sure he could do better. So he mixed corn starch with milk and grape jelly. That was good, too, but he wanted to see if he could do even better. After several weeks in his laboratory, he had still not invented the glue he was looking for. He called his friend Jefferson, who was working on the same problem in his own basement laboratory. Jefferson asked him which formula he had been working on. Richard realized then that he couldn't say exactly.

1. What information should Richard have recorded while he was working in his laboratory? _____

_____

2. Why should Richard have kept better records? _____

_____

_____

3. What would be a good method for keeping track of what Richard had tried?

_____

_____

4. How could Richard be sure he had communicated his information well?

_____

5. Can you think of any other way effective communication might have made Richard's experimentation easier? _____

_____

_____

_____

**Use with page A115.**

Name _____

Date _____

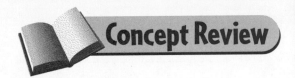

# How Do Plants Grow?

## Lesson Concept

Seeds contain embryo plants and stored food. Under the right conditions, seeds germinate. Seedlings are young plants that grow from the embryos. Some plants may reproduce asexually through vegetative propagation. Farmers and scientists use cross-pollination and grafting as other means of plant reproduction.

## Vocabulary

**embryo** (A116)          **cotyledons** (A116)          **germinate** (A118)

**seedling** (A118)          **vegetative propagation** (A119)          **grafting** (A120)

**tissue culture** (A120)

The following boxes make up a flowchart showing how a plant grows. Below the boxes you will find captions describing each part of the growth process. Put the letter of the correct caption in each box of the flowchart.

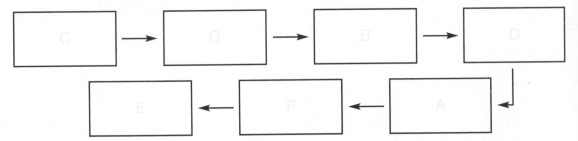

**A** As the root gets longer and thicker, a stem begins to emerge.

**B** Landing on moist, warm, fertile soil will allow the seed to take in moisture, to swell, and to germinate.

**C** The seed contains an embryo and stored food.

**D** The first part to emerge from the seed is the root.

**E** The seedling cannot yet make its own food but uses food stored in its cotyledons to grow.

**F** The seedling now has a well-developed root system, and its first leaves are producing food.

**G** The seed is dispersed by animals, wind, or water.

Name _____

Date _____

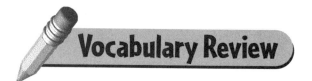

# Recognize Vocabulary

Listed below are scrambled vocabulary terms from Chapter 4. Use the clues to unscramble the terms. Write the unscrambled terms on the lines provided.

**1.** PIPOOSTORMTH

_____

a plant's response to light

**2.** PRECLURELINARSATOIL
(2 words)

_____

the process by which plants release energy in food to carry on life processes

**3.** FRANGITG

_____

a form of artificial reproduction that involves attaching branches from one plant to the branches of another plant

**4.** CEDOSTLOYN

_____

structures inside a seed that store food

**5.** ZELNITARITIOF

_____

the joining of a male reproductive cell with a female reproductive cell

**6.** EMISPIDER

_____

the single layer of cells on the surface of a leaf

**7.** AGREMETIN

_____

sprout

**8.** INSLEGED

_____

an embryo plant that has emerged from its seed and that is using energy from its cotyledons to grow

**9.** EMANSTS

_____

the parts of a flower that produce pollen

**10.** HISPETHONSOYTS

_____

the process by which plants make food

**11.** EVAPORATIONGIVETEPAGT
(2 words)

_____

the ability of some plants to reproduce without seeds

Use with pages A92–A127.

# Chapter 1 • Graphic Organizer for Chapter Concepts

## Cycles in Nature

# How Plants Use Carbon Dioxide

## Materials

safety goggles

2 beakers, 250 mL

water

funnel

dropper

bromothymol blue (BTB), an indicator solution

plastic straw

elodea

2 test tubes with caps

clock

CAUTION

## Activity Procedure

**1** **CAUTION** **Put on safety goggles, and leave them on until you complete Step 4.** Fill one beaker about two-thirds full of water. Use the dropper to add BTB to the water until you have a blue solution. BTB is an indicator. It changes color when carbon dioxide is present.

**2** **CAUTION** **Don't suck on the straw. If you do accidentally, don't swallow the solution. Spit it out, and rinse your mouth with water.** Put the plastic straw in the solution and blow into it. What do you **observe**? **Record** your observations.

My observations: _____

**3** Put the elodea into one test tube, and use the funnel to fill the tube with BTB solution from the beaker. Fill the other test tube with BTB solution only.

**4** Seal the test tubes with caps. Carefully turn the test tubes upside down, and place them in the empty beaker.

**5** Put the beaker containing the two test tubes in a sunny window for 1 hour. **Predict** what changes will occur in the test tubes. After 1 hour, **observe** both test tubes and **record** your observations.

**My prediction:** _____

_____

**My observations:** _____

_____

## Draw Conclusions

**1.** What changes did you **observe** in the BTB solution when you blew into it through the straw? Explain. It turned yellow because of the carbon dioxide blown into it.

**2.** What changes did you **observe** in the test tube of BTB after the elodea plant had been in it for 1 hour? It turned blue again.

**3.** **Compare** the color of the BTB solution in the test tube that had the elodea with the color of the BTB in the test tube that did not have the elodea. Describe any differences. The tube of BTB without the plant stayed yellow.

_____

**4.** **Scientists at Work** Scientists **observe** changes that happen during experiments. Then they **infer** what caused the changes. What can you infer about any changes that took place in the test tubes? Students may infer that the elodea used up the carbon dioxide.

**Investigate Further** What is the importance of sunlight in this investigation? **Hypothesize** about the importance of sunlight. Then **plan and conduct a simple investigation** to test your hypothesis.

**My hypothesis:** _____

_____

**My investigation design:** _____

_____

**My results:** _____

_____

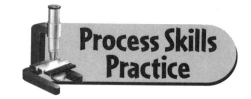

Process Skills
Practice

# Observe

Observing is a basic science skill. Making good observations will allow you to develop other important science skills, like inferring, comparing, classifying, and measuring.

## Think About Observing

Cecelia likes to grow tomatoes. She wanted to see if adding certain things to the soil would improve her tomato harvest. She treated different parts of her garden with kitchen-scrap compost, leaf-litter compost, and nitrogen fertilizer. Some parts of the garden were not treated. For five years she treated the soil and recorded the number of tomatoes produced by the plants in each area of her garden.

|  | Untreated Soil | Kitchen-Scrap Compost | Leaf-Litter Compost | Nitrogen Fertilizer |
|---|---|---|---|---|
| Year 1 | 130 | 145 | 140 | 165 |
| Year 2 | 125 | 155 | 155 | 155 |
| Year 3 | 110 | 160 | 165 | 155 |
| Year 4 | 95 | 155 | 170 | 145 |
| Year 5 | 70 | 165 | 180 | 150 |

1. Which treatment produced the best results over time? _____

2. Cecelia thought she should make a bar graph of her results. Do you think it would be easier to read her data this way? _____
   _____

3. What inference could you make about how Cecelia could improve the yield of plants grown in the untreated area of her garden? _____
   _____

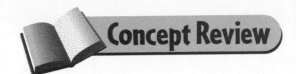

## Concept Review

# How Does Nature Reuse Materials?

Many of the materials organisms need are cycled through nature.

**Vocabulary**

| nitrogen cycle (B7) | carbon dioxide–oxygen cycle (B8) |
|---|---|

**Choose the correct caption from the table below each diagram, and write the appropriate letter below each picture.**

A _____   C _____   B _____

| **A** | Animal wastes and decaying organisms return nitrates and ammonia to the soil. |
|---|---|
| **B** | Animals get nitrogen by eating plants and other animals. |
| **C** | Plants make proteins from nitrogen in the soil. |

C _____   A _____   B _____

| **A** | Plants use carbon dioxide and release oxygen during photosynthesis. |
|---|---|
| **B** | Plants and animals use oxygen and release carbon dioxide during respiration. |
| **C** | Bacteria and fungi use as food some carbon from the tissues of dead animals. The rest is released as carbon dioxide. |

# Water, Water Everywhere

## Materials

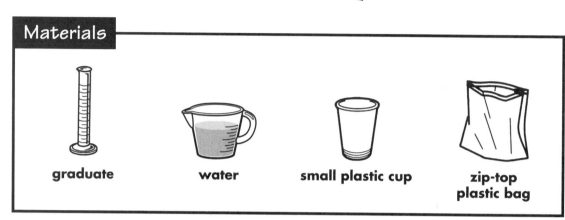

graduate　　　water　　　small plastic cup　　　zip-top plastic bag

## Activity Procedure

**1** Using the graduate, **measure** and pour 100 mL of water into the cup.

**2** Open the plastic bag, and carefully put the cup inside. Then seal the bag. Be careful not to spill any water from the cup.

**3** Place the sealed bag near a sunny window. **Predict** what will happen to the water in the cup.

**My prediction:** _____

**4** Leave the bag near a window for 3–4 days. **Observe** the cup and the bag each day. **Record** what you see.

**My observation:** _____

_____

**5** Remove the cup from the bag. **Measure** the amount of water in the cup by pouring it back into the graduate. **Calculate** any difference in the amount of water you poured into the cup and the amount of water you removed from the cup.

**My measurement:** _____

**My calculation:** _____

Name _____

## Draw Conclusions

1. What did you **observe** during the time the cup was inside the bag?
   Water drops appeared on the inside of the bag.

2. Where do you infer the water in the bag came from? Explain.
   From the cup; the amount of water poured out of the cup was less than the
   amount poured into the cup.

3. **Scientists at Work** Scientists often **infer** the cause of something they **observe**.
   What can you infer about the amount of water in the bag? The amount of
   water in the bag is the same as the amount of water missing from the cup.

**Investigate Further** How could you find out if the amount of water in the bag
is the same as the amount of water missing from the cup? Decide what equipment
you would need to use. Then **plan and conduct a simple investigation** that would
help you answer the question.

**My hypothesis:** _____

_____

**My investigation plan:** _____

_____

_____

**My results:** _____

Name _____

Date _____

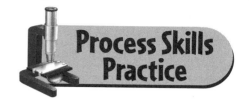

# Infer

When you infer, you draw conclusions to explain events.
Your inferences may not always be correct.

## Think About Inferring

1. Dion lives in a town with a lake nearby. People use the lake to swim, fish, and go boating. Dion reads in the newspaper that the rainfall in the area has been less than normal for the summer. When he went to the lake, he noticed that the water level in the lake was lower than usual for the time of year. What could Dion infer caused the water level in the lake to be below normal?

   _____

   _____

2. Since there had been little rain in Dion's town, people were told not to water their lawns. Many plants in Dion's yard and garden turned brown and died. But the big trees were still green and leafy. What could Dion infer caused some

   plants to die and the trees to survive? _____

   _____

   _____

3. Last year Dion's uncle Jeb had a house built outside Dion's town. Jeb built a deep well to pull water up into his house. This year Jeb was not able to get any water from his well. What could Jeb infer caused him to not get water from his

   well this year? _____

   _____

4. Jeb found out that he needs to dig his well deeper to get water. The county engineer explained to Jeb that many people built houses and drilled wells near Jeb. This caused the groundwater level to drop several feet when everyone started using their wells. The county engineer also told Jeb that his ground-water comes from an underground river. The lack of rain during the summer would not affect the groundwater level. Knowing this, tell whether your

   inference was correct in Question 3. _____

5. What does Question 4 show you about making inferences? _____

   _____

   _____

**Use with page B13.**

Name _____

Date _____

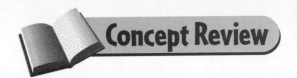

# Why Is the Water Cycle Important?

## Lesson Concept

Earth's water moves through the environment in the water cycle. All the water on Earth today is the same water that was here billions of years ago.

## Vocabulary

**water cycle** (B14)     **evaporation** (B14)     **condensation** (B14)

**precipitation** (B15)     **transpiration** (B15)

**Complete each sentence with a term from the list above.**

**1.** The sun's heat changes water at the surface of a lake to water vapor. This is called _____evaporation_____.

**2.** Water can move through the environment as liquid, vapor, or ice in the _____water cycle_____.

**3.** Water falls as _____precipitation_____ when clouds rise over a mountain.

**4.** Plants give off water through their stomata during _____transpiration_____.

**5.** High in the air, water changes into tiny droplets to form clouds. This process is called _____condensation_____.

**Write the numbers of the above sentences that would make the best captions for this picture.**

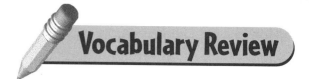

# Recognize Vocabulary

| | | |
|---|---|---|
| nitrogen cycle | water cycle | precipitation |
| transpiration | evaporation | condensation |
| carbon dioxide–oxygen cycle | | |

**Underline the vocabulary term that best completes each sentence.**

**1.** Heat changes liquid water into vapor during ____.

    **A** evaporation     **B** transpiration     **C** precipitation

**2.** The process in which plants give off water through their stomata is ____.

    **A** evaporation     **B** condensation     **C** transpiration

**3.** Gases needed for respiration are exchanged between organisms in

the ____ cycle.

    **A** nitrogen     **B** water     **C** carbon dioxide–oxygen

**4.** In the ____ cycle, bacteria fix a gas that plants and animals need for producing protein. Sometimes this gas comes from the air, and sometimes this gas comes from decaying organisms.

    **A** nitrogen     **B** water     **C** carbon dioxide–oxygen

**5.** Molecules in the ____ cycle can move through the environment as a solid, liquid, or gas.

    **A** nitrogen     **B** water     **C** carbon dioxide–oxygen

**6.** Water vapor changes to liquid during ____.

    **A** transpiration     **B** condensation     **C** precipitation

**7.** Water is moved from the atmosphere to Earth's surface during ____.

    **A** transpiration     **B** condensation     **C** precipitation

Use with pages B4–B17.

Chapter 2 • Graphic Organizer for Chapter Concepts

## Living Things Interact

Name _____

Date _____

# The Local Environment

## Materials

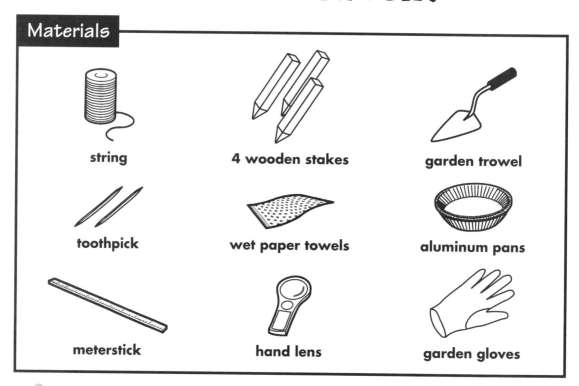

string

4 wooden stakes

garden trowel

toothpick

wet paper towels

aluminum pans

meterstick

hand lens

garden gloves

## CAUTION Activity Procedure

**1** **CAUTION** **Wear garden gloves to protect your hands.** Your teacher will send you to a grassy or lightly wooded area near your school. Once you are there, use the meterstick to **measure** an area of ground that is $1 \text{ m}^2$ (1 m × 1 m). Push a stake into each corner of the plot. Tie the string around the stakes.

**2** Before observing the plot, **predict** what living organisms and nonliving things you might find in this environment. **Record** your prediction.

My prediction: _____

**3** **Observe** the plot carefully. Use the hand lens to look for small things in the plot. **Record** your observations by making lists of the living organisms and the nonliving things in this environment.

My observations: _____

**4** Sit back and continue to **observe** the plot for a while. Look for living organisms, such as insects, interacting with other organisms or with the environment. Describe and **record** any interactions you observe.

My observations: _____

**5** Put wet paper towels in the aluminum pan, and use the garden trowel to scoop some soil onto them. Use a toothpick to sift through the soil. Be careful not to injure any living organisms with the toothpick.

**6** **Record** what you **observe**, especially any interactions. Then return the soil to the plot of ground.

**My observations:** _____

## Draw Conclusions

**1.** How did what you **predicted** compare with what you **observed**?

Answers will vary..Students may find fewer living organisms than they

predicted or more pieces of rock and trash.

_____

**2.** What did you **observe** that showed living organisms interacting with one another or with the environment? Answers will vary. Students may observe

such things as insects eating plants, worms moving soil, ants carrying bits of

trash, and so on.

_____

**3.** **Scientists at Work** Scientists often use prior knowledge to **predict** what they might find or what might happen. What prior knowledge did you use to predict what you would find in the plot of ground? Answers will vary.

Students may explain that they know that plants grow in soil, that insects eat

plants, and so on.

_____

**Investigate Further** Sometimes you can **infer** what interactions are occurring in an environment by **observing** what's in that environment. Choose an environment near your home or school. Observe what kinds of organisms live there, and infer how they interact with one another and with the environment.

_____

_____

_____

_____

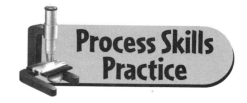
Process Skills
Practice

# Predict

Scientists use what they already know to predict what they may find or what may happen. Careful observation helps them make a prediction rather than a guess.

## Think About Predicting

Below is information about two different regions. Make predictions about the data by answering the questions that follow.

|  | Region I<br>Temperate Grasslands | Region II<br>Tropical Rain Forest |
|---|---|---|
| **Soil conditions** | porous soil, rich in organic matter | fragile soil |
| **Vegetation** | grasses and shrubs | tall, broad-leafed trees; multilevel canopy; sparse understory |
| **Climate** | short hot summers, long cold winters | tropical, hot throughout the year with rainy season |
| **Annual rainfall** | 25–75 cm (10–30 in.) | 200–400 cm (80–160 in.) |

1. In which region would you be more likely to find animals that graze on grasses? _____

2. In which region would you be more likely to find animals adapted to traveling along treetops? _____

3. Which region would you predict could recover more quickly after a fire? Explain your answer. _____

   _____

   _____

   _____

4. Predict which region would have the greater diversity of animals. Explain.

   _____

   _____

Name _____

Date _____

# What Are Ecosystems?

## Lesson Concept

An ecosystem consists of communities of living things and the environment in which they live.

## Vocabulary

| | | |
|---|---|---|
| **individual** (B28) | **population** (B28) | **community** (B28) |
| **ecosystem** (B28) | **habitat** (B29) | **niche** (B29) |

Use the vocabulary terms above as well as the terms listed below to complete the sentences about ecosystems.

| | | | |
|---|---|---|---|
| **temperature** | **survival** | **density** | **rainfall** |
| **soil conditions** | **plants** | **limiting factor** | |

1. A single organism in an environment is called an ____individual____.

2. A population has a role, or ____niche____, in its environment.

3. The sizes of animal populations are determined by the kinds and numbers of ____plants____ in an ecosystem.

4. Individuals of the same species make up a ____population____.

5. Populations of different organisms live together in a ____community____.

6. The ____soil conditions____, ____temperature____, and ____rainfall____ of an environment determine the types of plants that grow there.

7. In a healthy ecosystem, each population contributes to the ____survival____ of the other populations.

8. The amount of food is a ____limiting factor____ that affects population ____density____, or the number of individuals of a species in an ecosystem.

9. Communities and the environment make up an ____ecosystem____.

10. A ____habitat____ is a place where a population lives in an ecosystem.

# What Eats What In Ecosystems

## Materials

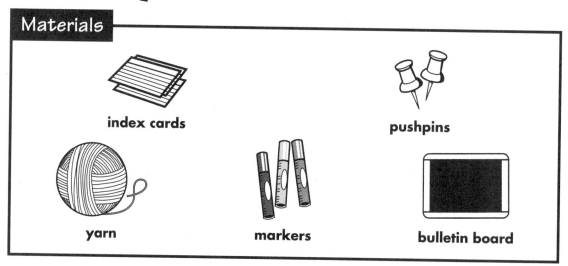

index cards

pushpins

yarn

markers

bulletin board

## Activity Procedure

**1** Your teacher will assign you an organism from a prairie ecosystem. Use an encyclopedia to find out what your organism eats. Then **classify** your organism into one of the following groups:

> plants
>
> meat-eating animals
>
> plant-eating animals
>
> animals that eat both plants and meat
>
> animals that eat dead organisms

**2** Use markers to draw your organism or write its name on an index card.

**3** Your teacher will now assign you to a class team. Each team will have at least one organism from each group listed above. With your teammates, **order** your team's cards to show what eats what in a prairie ecosystem.

**4** When your team's cards are in order, pin them in a line on the bulletin board. Connect the cards with yarn to show what eats what—both within your team's group of organisms and between those of other teams.

Name _____

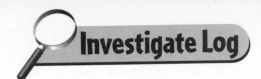
**Investigate Log**

## Draw Conclusions

**1.** When your team put its cards in **order**, what kind of organism was first?

plant

**2.** How would you **classify** the organism that came right after the first organism?

plant-eating animals or meat- and plant-eating animals

**3.** **Scientists at Work** When scientists **classify** things that happen in a particular order, it helps them understand how something works. Look again at your team's cards on the bulletin board. Could you classify or order them in any other way to explain what eats what in an ecosystem? Answers may vary, but students should realize that plants are always first in an ecosystem.

**Investigate Further** Find out what eats what in another ecosystem. If possible, use a computer to help you with your research. Then make a drawing to show the flow of energy in that ecosystem. Share your drawing with the class.

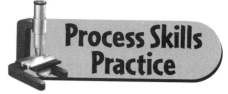

# Classify and Order

When you classify things, you put them into groups based on their similarities. When you order these groups, you can see relationships between the different groups.

## Think About Classifying and Ordering

1. Read the descriptions of four groups of organisms. Then use the numbers of the groups to classify the living things in the chart shown below.

**Group 1** eats foodmakers     **Group 3** eats animals

**Group 2** eats decaying things     **Group 4** makes its own food

| Living Things | Group |
|---|---|
| Plant-eating mice | |
| Grasses | |
| Bacteria that break down animal wastes and dead organisms | |
| Grass-eating voles | |
| Worms that eat decaying grasses and berries and waste products of animals | |
| Owls that eat weasels, mice, and voles | |
| Shrubs that produce berries | |
| Weasels that eat mice and voles | |

2. Order by what eats what from the living things listed. Start with the organism that doesn't eat anything. Use each of these living things only once.

*owl—grass—vole—waste-eating bacteria* _____

_____

3. Can you see another relationship between these groups other than what eats

what? _____

_____

_____

Name _____

Date _____

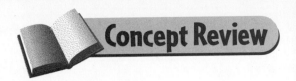

# How Does Energy Flow Through an Ecosystem?

## Lesson Concept

Energy starts to flow through an ecosystem when an organism uses the sun's energy to make food. Energy continues to flow when one organism eats another organism.

## Vocabulary

**producers** (B34)  **consumers** (B34)  **food chain** (B35)

**decomposer** (B35)  **food web** (B36)  **energy pyramid** (B38)

Below is an energy pyramid and a list of organisms. Write the names of the organisms where they belong on the energy pyramid.

**Grass**  **Lion**
**Vulture**  **Antelope**

4. __Vulture___

3. __Lion___

2. __Antelope___

1. __Grass___

5. If a producer makes 1000 units of energy, how many units of this energy can a third-level consumer use?

   _1 unit of energy_____

6. What does it mean to say that an organism is a producer? __An organism can make its own food.__

7. First-level consumers are called __herbivores_____, while second- and third-level consumers are called __carnivores_____.

8. Is the energy pyramid more like a food chain or a food web? Explain.

   _It is more like a food chain because it shows only one set of organisms consuming each other. No organism is consumed by more than one other organism._

9. What kind of organism connects both ends of a food chain? __a decomposer__

Use with page B39.

Name _____

Date _____

# Body Color

## Materials

colored acetate
sheets: red, blue,
green, yellow

hole
punch

large
green
cloth

clock with
second
hand

## Activity Procedure

1 Use the table on the next page. Use the hole punch to make 50 pieces from each of the acetate sheets. These colored acetate pieces will stand for insects that a bird is hunting.

2 **Predict** which color would be the easiest to find in grass. Predict which would be the hardest to find. **Record** your predictions.

My predictions: _____

3 Spread the cloth on the floor. Your teacher will randomly scatter the acetate "insects" over the cloth.

4 Each member of the group should kneel at the edge of the cloth. You will each try to pick up as many colored acetate "insects" as you can in 15 seconds. You must pick them up one at a time.

5 Total the number of acetate pieces of each color your group collected. **Record** the data in the table.

6 Put aside the "insects" you collected. Repeat Step 4 two more times. After each 15-second "hunt," **record** the number of acetate pieces of each color your group collected. After the third hunt, total each column.

Name _____

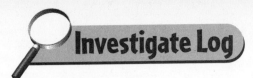 

| | Number of Insects Found | | | |
|---|---|---|---|---|
| | **Red** | **Blue** | **Green** | **Yellow** |
| Hunt 1 | | | | |
| Hunt 2 | | | | |
| Hunt 3 | | | | |
| Totals | | | | |

## Draw Conclusions

**1.** Look at the data you **recorded** for each hunt. What color of acetate was collected least? _Answers may vary, but green will probably be the least collected color for the first trial._

Were the results of each hunt the same, or were they different? Explain. _The number of green pieces collected will probably increase with each trial._

**2.** **Compare** the results with what you **predicted**. Do the results match your prediction? Explain. _Answers will vary, but students probably predicted that green insects would be the hardest to see and collect._

**3.** **Scientists at Work** Scientists often **gather data** before they **infer** a relationship between things. Based on the data you gathered, what can you infer about the survival chances of brown-colored insects in areas where grasses and leaves turn brown in the fall? _Students should infer that brown insects would blend in with brown grass and leaves and have a better chance to survive._

**Investigate Further** Many insects have a body shape that allows them to blend in with their background. **Hypothesize** about what body shape might help an insect hide in a dead tree. Then **plan and conduct a simple investigation** to test your hypothesis.

**My hypothesis:** _____

**My plan:** _____

**My results:** _____
_____

Name _____

Date _____

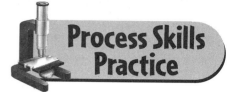

# Gather Data and Infer

One way to gather data is to observe objects or events. You can use the data to make inferences. You may need to gather more data to decide if your inference is correct.

## Think About Gathering Data and Inferring

Abdul learned that periwinkles, small shelled organisms similar to snails, cling to rocks near the ocean shoreline. He spent a day at the shoreline gathering data about periwinkles on one cliff. He observed four types of periwinkles that were clinging to different levels of the cliff. He made a table to show the number of each type at each level.

| Cliff Level | Periwinkle Type | | | |
|---|---|---|---|---|
| | Large Pink | Medium Blue | Small Pink | Large Gray |
| Splash zone (above or at high-tide level) | 0 | 2 | 8 | 0 |
| Upper shore (under water 6–12 hr a day) | 1 | 5 | 3 | 3 |
| Middle shore (under water 12–18 hr a day) | 4 | 3 | 0 | 7 |
| Lower shore (under water 18–24 hr a day) | 7 | 1 | 0 | 1 |

1. What can Abdul infer about the lower shore? _____

_____

2. What inference can Abdul make about the splash zone? _____

_____

3. What can Abdul infer about the different sizes of periwinkles on the cliff?

_____

_____

4. What other data could Abdul gather to support inferences he made?

_____

_____

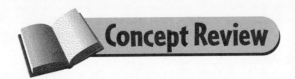

# How Do Organisms Compete and Survive in an Ecosystem?

## Lesson Concept

Organisms have various ways to compete for limited resources in ecosystems.

## Vocabulary

| | |
|---|---|
| **competition** (B42) | **symbiosis** (B45) |
| **instinct** (B46) | **learned behavior** (B46) |

**Fill in the chart below about how these organisms survive in their ecosystems.**
Accept reasonable answers. The italicized answers below are discussed in the book.

| Canada Goose | Cheetah | Raccoon |
|---|---|---|
| *(bird image)* | *(cheetah image)* | *(raccoon image)* |
| **Resource It Must Share or For Which It Must Compete** | | |
| *grains, water plants* | *zebras and antelopes* | *sea turtles' eggs* |
| **Adaptation That Helps It Compete** | | |
| *body parts for flying* | *high speed for hunting* | *has paws to handle objects* |
| **Instinct** | | |
| *mating for life, building shelters, migrating, eating grains and water plants* | *hunting prey, finding mates* | *finding mates, building shelter* |
| **Behavior It Might Learn** | | |
| *hunting* | *hunting* | *hunting* |

Name _____

Date _____

# Vanishing Habitats

graph paper

globe or world map

calculator

graphing calculator
or computer (optional)

| Rain Forest Area and Human Population In Ecuador | | | | |
|---|---|---|---|---|
| Year | 1961 | 1971 | 1981 | 1991 |
| Rain forest (square km) | 173,000 | 153,000 | No data | 112,000 |
| Population (in millions) | 5.162 | 7.035 | No data | 10.782 |

## Activity Procedure

**1** Locate Ecuador, a country in South America, on the globe or world map.

**2** Study the table above. It shows the size of Ecuador's rain forests and the size of its human population between 1961 and 1991.

**3** **Calculate** and **record** the changes in rain forest area for each period shown (1961–1971 and 1971–1991). Then calculate and record the changes in the population size for the same periods.

**4** Using graph paper and a pencil, a graphing calculator, or a computer, make a double-bar graph that shows changes in forest area and population size for these periods.

Name _____

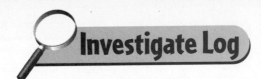

## Draw Conclusions

1. **Compare** the two sets of data in the double-bar graph. What relationship, if any, do you **observe** between the growth of the human population and the amount of rain forest in Ecuador? As the human population increases, forest area decreases.

2. Based on the **data collected**, what can you **infer** about the size of Ecuador's human population and the area of its rain forests in 1981? In 1981, human population was about 8.909 million and the forest area was about 132,500 km².

3. According to the data, what do you **predict** the size of the rain forests in Ecuador will be in 2001 if the human population increases at the same rate as it has in the past? In 2001 the forest area should be about 92,000 km².

4. **Scientists at Work** Scientists often **interpret data** to help them **infer** what may happen. If the size of the rain-forest habitat keeps getting smaller, what can you infer about the populations of animals that live there? Further loss of habitat could lead to smaller populations of animals living in the rain forest.

**Investigate Further** Research the changes in the size of the human population over several decades in your area. Then make a graph of the changes. **Infer** how these changes in the human population might have affected animal populations in your area.

Name _____

Date _____

# Interpret Data

Interpreting data involves using other skills, such as predicting and hypothesizing, to explain patterns or relationships in data. Interpretations may change when additional data is obtained.

## Think About Interpreting Data

The table shows the number of individuals of different populations in two similar regions. Both regions were forests in 1995. Both became the sites of housing developments in 1999. On one site a network of forest areas was left between house lots. On the other site all the trees were removed, houses were built, and each lot was individually landscaped.

| Forest Areas Left | | | Newly Landscaped | | |
|---|---|---|---|---|---|
| | 1995 | 2000 | | 1995 | 2000 |
| Owl | 8 | 4 | Owl | 9 | 1 |
| Bobcat | 5 | 0 | Bobcat | 4 | 0 |
| Fox | 11 | 7 | Fox | 11 | 4 |
| Beaver | 7 | 2 | Beaver | 7 | 0 |
| Rabbit | 28 | 35 | Rabbit | 24 | 40 |
| Deer | 6 | 9 | Deer | 7 | 12 |
| Skunk | 4 | 7 | Skunk | 4 | 9 |

1. Which populations decreased at both sites? _____

2. Which populations increased at both sites? _____

3. How do you explain the different impacts of the housing developments on the populations that increased and the populations that decreased?

_____

_____

4. How would you use this data for planning another housing development?

_____

_____

_____

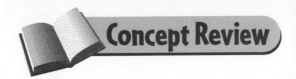

WB87

# What Is Extinction and What Are Its Causes?

## Lesson Concept

Extinction occurs when the last individual of a species dies. Extinction can happen naturally or be caused by human activities.

## Vocabulary

**extinct** (B51)          **endangered** (B51)          **threatened** (B51)

**Fill in the missing part in each cause-and-effect chain below. One column starts a sentence, while the other finishes the sentence.**

| Cause | Effect |
|---|---|
| **1.** Building new roads, homes, or buildings | reduces the size of a natural habitat. |
| **2.** A volcano or hurricane | can destroy an island habitat naturally. |
| **3.** Drought | kills producers in a food chain naturally. |
| Importing exotic species | **4.** brings diseases that kill native populations. |
| Strict hunting laws | **5.** may bring back populations of threatened or endangered species. |
| A change in an island habitat | **6.** may be permanent because there may be no other populations to replace lost organisms. |
| Using DDT in the 1940s | **7.** weakened bald eagle eggshells, causing fewer eagles to hatch. The bald eagle and peregrine falcon became endangered. |
| Restoring and saving peregrine falcon habitats has | **8.** increased the peregrine falcon population and removed it from the endangered species list. |

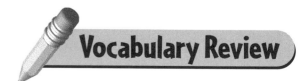
# Recognize Vocabulary

Write the letter of the definition in the right-hand column in the
space in front of the term that it matches in the left-hand column.

_____ 1. producers

_____ 2. population

_____ 3. food web

_____ 4. consumers

_____ 5. habitat

_____ 6. exotic

_____ 7. competition

_____ 8. energy pyramid

_____ 9. learned behaviors

_____ 10. decomposer

_____ 11. community

_____ 12. ecosystem

_____ 13. threatened

_____ 14. individual

_____ 15. instinct

_____ 16. food chain

_____ 17. niche

_____ 18. endangered

_____ 19. symbiosis

_____ 20. extinct

A role of a population of organisms within a particular habitat

B community of organisms and their physical environment

C individuals of the same kind living in the same environment

D shows the relationships between many different food chains in a single ecosystem

E contest between organisms for limited resources

F species become this after the last individual in the population dies

G place in an ecosystem where each population lives

H consumer that breaks down tissues of decaying organisms

I all the populations of organisms living together in an environment

J behaviors animals are taught or acquire after birth

K living things that must eat to get energy

L single organism in an environment

M behavior an organism inherits

N likely to become endangered if it is not protected

O organisms that produce their own food through photosynthesis

P shows amount of energy available to pass from one level of a food chain to the next

Q shows how consumers in an ecosystem are connected to one another according to what they eat

R nonnative organisms

S having a population so small it is likely to disappear unless steps are taken to save it

T long-term relationship between different kinds of organisms

# Chapter 3 • Graphic Organizer for Chapter Concepts

## Biomes

### LESSON 1
### LAND BIOMES

Types

1. Tropical Rainforest _____
2. Deciduous Forest _____
3. Taiga _____
4. Grassland _____
5. Desert _____
6. Tundra _____

### LESSON 2
### WATER BIOMES

Types

1. Intertidal Zone _____
2. Near-shore Zone _____
3. Open-ocean Zone _____
4. Estuaries _____

Name _____

Date _____

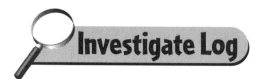

# Biomes and Climates

## Materials

**map of North American climate zones**

**map of North American biomes**

**markers or colored pencils**

## Activity Procedure

**1** On the map of North American climate zones, color the different climates as shown in the table below.

| North American Climate Zones | | |
|:---:|:---|:---:|
| **Area** | **Climate** | **Color** |
| 1 | More than 250 cm rain; warm all year | green |
| 2 | 75–250 cm rain or snow; warm summer, cold winter | purple |
| 3 | 20–60 cm rain or snow; cool summer, cold winter | blue |
| 4 | 10–40 cm rain or snow; warm summer, cold winter | orange |
| 5 | Less than 10 cm rain; hot summer, cool winter | yellow |
| 6 | 250 cm snow (25 cm rain); cold all year | brown |

**2** On the map of North American biomes, color the biomes as shown in the chart on the next page.

Name _____

| North American Biomes | | |
|---|---|---|
| **Area** | **Biome** | **Color** |
| A | Tropical rain forest | green |
| B | Deciduous forest | purple |
| C | Taiga | blue |
| D | Grassland | orange |
| E | Desert | yellow |
| F | Tundra | brown |

**❸ Compare** the green areas on the two maps. How does the area with a warm, wet climate compare to the area of tropical rain forest? Compare other biomes and climate zones that are colored alike.

## Draw Conclusions

1. How do areas on the climate map **compare** to areas shown in the same color on the biome map? Areas on the climate map are very similar in size and shape to areas on the biome map.

2. **Observe** the maps. If an area is too wet to be a desert but too dry to be a forest, what biome would you expect to find there? grassland

3. **Order** the biomes from wettest to driest. tropical rain forest, deciduous forest, taiga, grassland, desert, tundra

4. **Scientists at Work** When scientists **compare** sets of data, they can **draw conclusions** about relationships between the data sets. Conifers are dominant plants of the taiga. Broad-leaved trees are the dominant plants of the deciduous forest. What conclusions can you draw about the water needs of conifers compared to those of broad-leaved trees? Taiga gets 20–60 cm of rain or snow; deciduous forest gets 75–250 cm of rain or snow. Conifers need less water than deciduous trees.

**Investigate Further** Use a computer to make a chart showing the climates of the six biomes and a map combining climate zones and biomes.

Name _____

Date _____

# Compare

When you compare, you identify ways objects or events are similar or different.

## Think About Comparing

Jessica made a chart to compare three different biomes in the United States.

|  | Desert | Deciduous Forest | Grassland |
|---|---|---|---|
| Climate | hot and dry summers, warm and dry winters | warm summers, cold winters, plenty of rain | hot summers with little rain; warm, wet springs and falls; cold winters |
| Vegetation | slow-growing plants that conserve water, like cacti and thorny shrubs | mostly trees and shrubs that shed leaves in fall, some grasses and flowers | mostly fast-growing grasses, some flowers, a few shrubs and trees |
| Animal adaptations | move to warmer or cooler locations during temperature changes, conserve water | hide in vegetation, fur is shed in spring and thickens before winter | can burrow or move fast, fur is shed in spring and thickens before winter, some can travel far |

1. Which two regions have similar vegetation? Explain. _____

_____

_____

2. Jessica notices that grassland and forest animals have different ways of escaping danger. Why would animals need to run fast on grassland but hide in a forest?

_____

_____

3. Jessica knows that the fur of grassland animals grows thicker in winter. How do you think the thickness of fur on grassland animals that moved to a warmer place in the winter compares to the fur of animals that didn't move? Explain.

_____

_____

Name _____

Date _____

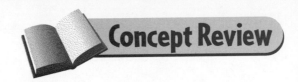

# What Are Land Biomes?

## Lesson Concept

A biome is a large-scale ecosystem. There are many kinds of biomes, each with a different climate and organisms that have adaptations to live in it.

## Vocabulary

| | |
|---|---|
| **biome** (B64) | **climate zone** (B64) |

**Read the descriptions of the biomes below, and name each type of biome.**

You'll find several layers of plants here. In the fall, people come to see the pretty leaves.

1. deciduous forests _____

Grains that feed people and animals grow here.

2. grasslands _____

It can be very hot during the day and very cold at night.

3. desert _____

The trees are green year-round here. It is cold and has many mosquitoes.

4. taiga _____

When it's dark up here, everything is white.

5. tundra _____

Half of Earth's varieties of plant life are found here.

6. rain forest _____

# Life in a Pond Community

## Materials

**Microslide Viewer**

**Microslide set of pond life**

**Microslide set of ocean life**

## Alternate Materials

**pond water**

**hand lens**

**dropper**

**slide**

**coverslip**

**microscope**

## Activity Procedure

**Note: If microscopes are available, your teacher may provide an alternate procedure that you will follow to make a slide and observe a drop of pond water.**

**1** Put the "Pond Life" Microslide in the Microslide Viewer. **Observe** the first photograph, which shows the fish and plants found in a pond. **Record** your observations by making a drawing and writing a short description of these organisms. You may use the information on the Microslide card to help you with your description.

**2** The other photographs in the set show microscopic life in a pond. **Observe** each of the organisms. Then **record** your observations by making a drawing and writing a short description of each organism.

**3** **Classify** each of the organisms as producer or consumer. **Record** this information on your drawings and in your descriptions.

**4** Now put the "Marine Biology" Microslide in the Microslide Viewer. **Observe** each of the organisms, but don't read the information on the Microslide card yet. **Predict** which of the organisms are producers and which are consumers.

My prediction: _____

**5** Now read the information on the Microslide card to see if your predictions were correct.

## Draw Conclusions

1. **Compare** the two sets of organisms. Which pond organism was similar to the coral polyp? Which marine organisms were similar to the algae?
   the hydra; the phytoplankton

2. In what way were all the producers alike? They were all green. (They all had chlorophyll.)

3. **Scientists at Work** Scientists often **infer** relationships between organisms after they **observe** them in their natural habitats. Think about your observations of pond life and ocean life. What organisms in a pond community have the same position in a pond food chain as zooplankton has in an ocean food chain?
   amoeba and paramecium

**Investigate Further** Now that you have observed photographs of pond organisms, use the materials in the *Alternate Materials* list to **observe** a drop of water from a pond or other water ecosystem. Then **classify** as producers or consumers the organisms you observe. See page R5 for tips on using a microscope.

# Infer

Inferring involves using logical reasoning to draw conclusions from observations.

## Think About Inferring

Vladimir and his family just moved into their new home in Arkansas. He wrote a letter to his cousin Victor. In the letter he described the pond behind his home.

---

June 18
Dear Victor,

I love our new home! When you visit, we can go swimming in the pond behind our house. Today would be great for swimming. It's a hot, sunny day. It's 2:00 in the afternoon, and the thermometer says it's 82° Fahrenheit.

I'm looking out at the pond. I can see plants with roots in pond mud. They have long, thin stems and large, flat leaves floating on the pond's surface. Along the shore are clumps of tall grasslike plants with blades about a meter high. Lots of small bugs with long jointed legs walk on the surface of the water, more easily than I walk on the sidewalk. In the middle of the pond, six turtles are sitting on a log in a sunny spot. A female duck with five ducklings behind her is swimming by the turtles. I can hear buzzing and whirring from all the insects nearby.

I can't wait for your visit. Don't forget to bring your swim trunks!

Your cousin,
Vladimir

---

1. Victor knows that plants need to get sunlight to survive. What could Victor infer about the pond plants Vladimir observed? _____

    _____

    _____

2. Vladimir mentioned that many insects were walking on the pond's surface. Should Victor infer that the pond's surface where the insects were walking was calm or wavy? Explain. _____

    _____

3. Victor is coming to see Vladimir in five weeks. What could Victor infer about what the pond will be like at that time? _____

    _____

    _____

Name _____

Date _____

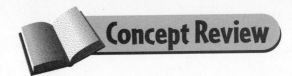

# What Are Water Ecosystems?

## Lesson Concept

Water ecosystems occur in fresh, salt, and brackish water.

## Vocabulary

| | |
|---|---|
| **intertidal zone** (B77) | **near-shore zone** (B77) |
| **open-ocean zone** (B77) | **estuary** (B80) |

Use the terms below to label the parts of the picture.

| | | |
|---|---|---|
| **fresh water** | **open-ocean zone** | **intertidal zone** |
| **near-shore zone** | **estuary** | |

fresh water

near-shore zone

estuary

intertidal zone

open-ocean zone

6. Where do near-shore zones get their nutrients and in what form are these nutrients? Rivers that empty into the ocean dump dead organisms onto the ocean floor.

_____

_____

7. Name three important roles of estuaries. They provide habitats for many organisms. Two-thirds of the world's fish and shellfish are harvested from estuaries. They prevent coastal flooding. They prevent shoreline erosion.

_____

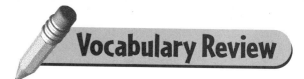
# Recognize Vocabulary

| | | |
|---|---|---|
| biome | climate zone | intertidal zone |
| near-shore zone | open-ocean zone | estuary |

Use the clues below to fill in the puzzle with the vocabulary terms.

**Across**

**3.** a saltwater ecosystem with calm waters; most nutrients provided by rivers

**4.** a place with similar yearly patterns of temperature, rainfall, and amount of sunlight

**6.** a large-scale ecosystem

**Down**

**1.** a saltwater ecosystem where breaking waves provide oxygen and nutrients

**2.** a saltwater ecosystem with very deep water

**5.** where a freshwater river empties into the ocean

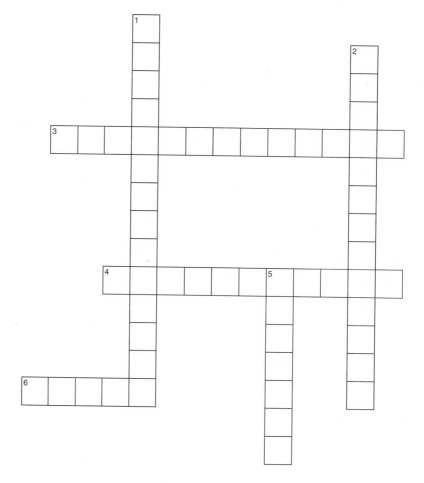

Use with pages B62–B81.

Chapter 4 • Graphic Organizer for Chapter Concepts

## Protecting and Preserving Ecosystems

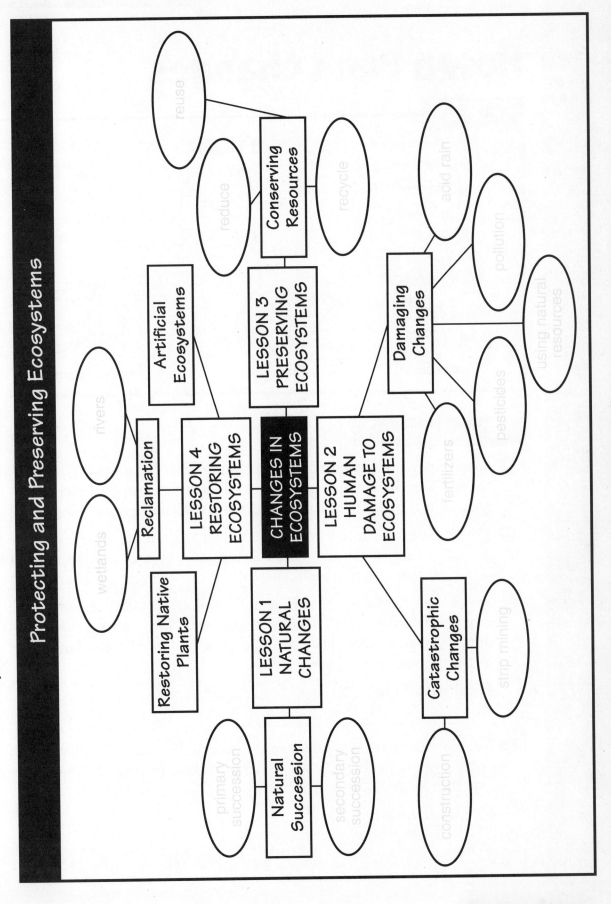

reuse

Conserving Resources

reduce

recycle

acid rain

Artificial Ecosystems

LESSON 3 PRESERVING ECOSYSTEMS

Damaging Changes

pollution

using natural resources

pesticides

rivers

Reclamation

LESSON 4 RESTORING ECOSYSTEMS

CHANGES IN ECOSYSTEMS

LESSON 2 HUMAN DAMAGE TO ECOSYSTEMS

fertilizers

wetlands

Restoring Native Plants

LESSON 1 NATURAL CHANGES

Catastrophic Changes

strip mining

primary succession

Natural Succession

secondary succession

construction

# How a Pond Changes

## Materials

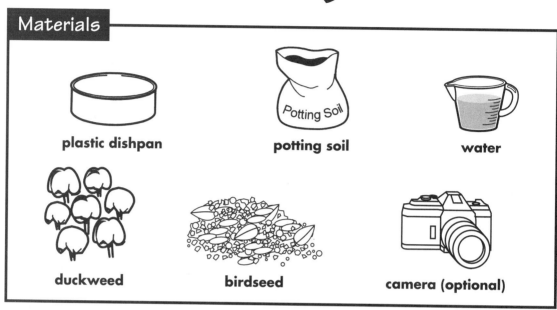

plastic dishpan     potting soil     water

duckweed     birdseed     camera (optional)

## Activity Procedure

1. Spread a layer of potting soil about 5 cm deep in the dishpan. Now bank the soil about 10 cm high around the edges of the dishpan. Leave a low spot, with about 1 cm of soil, in the center of the pan.

2. Slowly pour water into the low area of the pan until the water is about 4 cm deep. You may have to add more water as some of it soaks into the soil. Place some duckweed on the "pond."

3. Sprinkle birdseed over the surface of the soil. Don't worry if some of the seed falls into the water. Do not water the seed. Take a photograph or draw a picture to **record** how your pond looks. Put your pond model in a sunny window.

   **My observations:** _____

   _____

4. After three or four days, **measure** and **record** the depth of the water. Take another photograph, or draw another picture. Then sprinkle more birdseed over the soil. Water the soil lightly.

   **My measurement:** _____

Name _____

**5** After three or four more days,
**observe** how your pond has changed. **Measure** and **record** the depth of the water. **Compare** your observations with the photographs you took or the pictures you drew.

**My measurement:** _____

**My comparisons:** _____

_____

_____

## Draw Conclusions

**1.** Describe any changes in the pond during the week. How did the depth of the water change? Possible answers: The seed sprouted; much of the "pond" dried up; the pond filled in with dirt and seeds; the duckweed covered the pond.

**2.** **Compare** the changes in your model with those in a real pond. How are they the same? In both the model and a real pond, soil washes into the pond, the water dries up if there isn't any rain, and plants begin to grow at the edge of the pond.

How are they different? This process occurs much more slowly in a real pond.

**3.** **Scientists at Work** By **observing** the changes that occur while **they use models**, scientists can **infer** changes that might occur in nature. From what you observed in your model, what do you infer might happen to a real pond over time? A real pond might get smaller and eventually disappear as the water evaporates, the pond fills with soil, and plants begin to grow.

**Investigate Further** An actual pond ecosystem has a greater diversity of plants and animals than your model. **Make another model** that includes a greater variety of living things.

# Use Models and Infer

When objects are very big or very small, or when processes take a long time or do not happen often, a mental or physical model can help you understand the process. You can use observations of models to make inferences.

## Think About Using Models and Inferring

While planting a vegetable garden in his backyard, Mr. Koumjian decided to make a model of a region that has undergone a natural disaster. He did this by turning over the soil in one corner of the garden and leaving it unplanted. He wondered what would happen to this patch of soil if he didn't do anything to it. The garden was surrounded by a grass lawn. There were berry bushes and honeysuckle vines in another part of the yard, along with two apple trees and two pear trees.

1. Is Mr. Koumjian's garden patch a good model for an area left after a fire? Why or why not? _____

   _____

   _____

2. Is Mr. Koumjian's garden patch a good model for an area left after a flood? Why or why not? _____

3. Is Mr. Koumjian's garden patch a good model for an area left after a volcanic eruption? Why or why not? _____

   _____

   _____

4. How long will Mr. Koumjian have to observe his model to see the changes that occur in an area after a natural disaster? _____

   _____

   _____

5. Why do you think Mr. Koumjian chose to make this model instead of going to a place where there had been a natural disaster? _____

   _____

   _____

   _____

# How Do Ecosystems Change Naturally?

## Lesson Concept

Slow changes occur naturally in ecosystems every day. Quick changes, like fires, also occur naturally.

## Vocabulary

**succession** (B92)    **pioneer plants** (B92)    **climax community** (B93)

**Use the vocabulary terms above to complete the captions.**

**A** Alder and willow trees can take root now. These trees have relatively slender trunks and grow quickly. They also add acids to the soil.

**B** Now the soil is deep enough to support the tall, sturdy hemlock and spruce trees. These trees are the _____climax community_____. If left undisturbed, this forest could stay almost the same for thousands of years.

**C** Grasses and flowering plants begin to take root. The thick root structure of these plants anchors the soil as it deepens. These plants also attract insects, birds, worms, and small mammals that add wastes to the soil.

**D** In the early stages of _____succession_____, lichens form a thin layer of soil, which allows moss, a _____pioneer plant_____, to grow. Bits of organic matter and bird droppings become trapped in dense moss and add more nutrients to the deepening soil.

**Write the letter of the caption above that goes with each picture below.**

**1.** ___D___    **2.** ___C___    **3.** ___A___    **4.** ___B___

# How Chemical Fertilizer Affects a Pond

## Materials

4 jars or cups with lids

marker

pond water

dropper

liquid fertilizer

## Activity Procedure

**1** Use the marker to label the jars 1, 2, 3, and 4.

**2** Fill the jars with pond water.

**3** Put 10 drops of liquid fertilizer in Jar 1, 20 drops in Jar 2, and 40 drops in Jar 3. Don't put any fertilizer in Jar 4.

**4** Put the lids on the jars. Then place the jars in a sunny window.

**5** **Observe** the jars every day for two weeks. **Record** your observations.

My observations: _____

_____

_____

_____

_____

Name _____

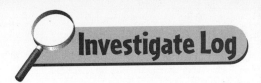 

## Draw Conclusions

**1.** What differences did you **observe** among the jars? Which jar had the most plant growth? Which had the least plant growth? How could you tell?

The jar with the most fertilizer had the most growth. The jar with no fertilizer

had the least growth. The jar with the most growth is very green and cloudy.

**2.** As organisms die and decay, they use up the oxygen in the water. Which jar do you **infer** will eventually have the least oxygen? Students should infer that the

jar with the most growth will eventually have the least oxygen.

**3.** When water ecosystems are contaminated by fertilizer, fish and other animal populations begin to die off. Why do you think this happens?

There is not enough oxygen in the water for the fish and other animals

to breathe.

**4.** **Scientists at Work** When scientists **identify and control variables**, they can **observe** the effects of one variable at a time. What variable were you observing the effect of in this investigation? the amount of fertilizer in the water

What variables did you control? Possible answers include: size of water

sample, type of water sample, amount of sunlight, and length of time sample

sat in sunlight. Students may suggest others.

**Investigate Further** Some fertilizers contain additional chemicals that are supposed to kill weeds. **Predict** the effects of using these chemicals on a lawn. Then **plan and conduct a simple investigation** to test your prediction.

**My plan:** _____

_____

_____

**My observations:** _____

_____

_____

**My results:** _____

_____

_____

_____

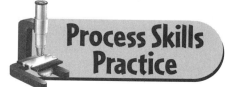

# Identify and Control Variables

When you identify variables in an experiment, you pick out the factors that can be changed in a situation. You control variables in an experiment by changing one of the variables and keeping all the others the same.

## Think About Identifying and Controlling Variables

Read the descriptions of each of the experiments below. Then, on the line below the description, identify the variables that affect the outcome of the experiment.

**1.** Fill each of three 1-quart glass jars with 2 inches of clay, 2 inches of sand, and 2 inches of potting soil. Put four earthworms in one jar, four ants in another jar, and no animals in the third jar. Observe the jars every day for a week. Make notes about the ways the contents of the jars change or stay the same. What is the variable in this experiment and what could you learn by controlling it?

_____

_____

**2.** Fill two aluminum baking pans of the same size with a layer of potting soil 3 inches deep. Plant grass seed in one of the pans. Place both pans in a sunny location, and water both pans with the same amount of water every two days. After the grass has grown to a height of 3 inches, prop up one end of both pans on a block or brick 1 to 2 inches high. (Both pans should be propped up on blocks of the same height.) Then place an empty pan in front of the lower end of each pan containing soil. Slowly pour one half-gallon of water into the higher end of each pan. Measure how much water and soil runs off into each of the empty pans. What is the variable in this experiment, and what could you

learn by controlling it? _____

**3.** Place four identical leafy green houseplants in a sunny spot. Each plant should be in a 2-inch pot, be the same height (about 4 inches), and have about the same number and size of leaves. Label the pots *A*, *B*, *C*, and *D*. Water each pot with 8 ounces of water every day. Water Plant A with plain water. Add 1 teaspoon of distilled white vinegar to the water for Plant B every day. Add 1 tablespoon of distilled white vinegar to the water for Plant C every day. Add 3 tablespoons of distilled white vinegar to the water for Plant D every day. Observe the plants each day, making notes on their appearances. What is the variable in this experiment, and what could you learn by controlling it?

_____

_____

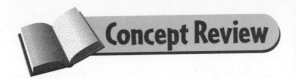

# How Do People Change Ecosystems?

## Lesson Concept

Human activity can change ecosystems. Some ecosystems can recover from the changes, while other ecosystems are altered forever.

## Vocabulary

| pollution (B99) | acid rain (B99) |
| --- | --- |

**Complete the sentences below by writing the letter of a phrase from the chart.**

| | | | |
| --- | --- | --- | --- |
| **A** | paper products damage forest ecosystems and destroy habitats | **E** | corn, barley, wheat, or oats reduces the diversity of life |
| **B** | nitrogen oxides and sulfur dioxide that mix with water vapor and cause acid rain | **F** | strip mining, all the communities and many nonliving parts of an ecosystem are destroyed |
| **C** | roads, homes, schools, and office buildings, habitats for other organisms are destroyed | **G** | destroy habitats completely or change conditions so much that natural communities can't survive |
| **D** | kill unwanted plant and animal pests can damage natural ecosystems | **H** | birds, fish, and other water animals |

**1.** Replacing the natural producers in a grassland ecosystem with _____ E _____.

**2.** Using pesticides and herbicides to _____ D _____.

**3.** As human communities grow and people build _____ C _____.

**4.** Cutting down trees to make wood and _____ A _____.

**5.** Energy stations and motor vehicles give off _____ B _____ .

**6.** Runoff from acid rain kills _____ H _____.

**7.** When topsoil and rock layers are removed in the process of _____ F _____.

**8.** Large-scale construction projects on fragile ecosystems may _____ G _____.

Use with page B101.

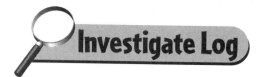
# What Happens in a Landfill

## Materials

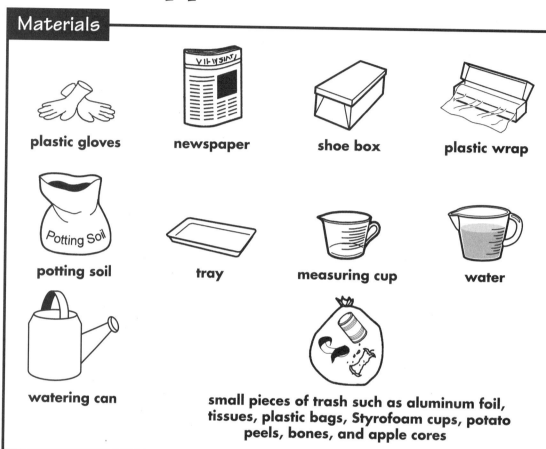

plastic gloves

newspaper

shoe box

plastic wrap

potting soil

tray

measuring cup

water

watering can

small pieces of trash such as aluminum foil, tissues, plastic bags, Styrofoam cups, potato peels, bones, and apple cores

**CAUTION** ## Activity Procedure

1. Make a chart listing ten different items of trash. Allow space in your chart to **record** observations you will make later.

2. **CAUTION** **Put on the plastic gloves.** Spread newspaper on your work surface. Choose the ten items of trash listed on your chart to put in the model landfill. Lay the trash on the newspaper.

3. Now prepare the model landfill. First, line the shoe box with plastic wrap. Then put a layer of potting soil on the bottom of the box.

4. Take the pieces of trash from the newspaper and place them on top of the soil. Then cover the trash completely with another layer of soil.

5. Set the model landfill on the tray. Use the watering can to sprinkle the surface of the soil each day with 50 mL of water.

**6** After two weeks, put on plastic gloves and remove the top layer of soil. **Observe** the items of trash, and **record** your observations.

**My observations:** _____

_____

_____

## Draw Conclusions

1. Did you **observe** anything starting to decay? What items decayed the most? What items decayed the least? Animal and plant matter decays quickly. Plastics and aluminum do not decay at all.

2. Things that decay are said to be *biodegradable*. What items in your trash are biodegradable? plant and animal matter and paper

3. What do you **infer** might eventually happen to trash that is not biodegradable? Nothing, because it would never decay.

4. **Scientists at Work** Scientists often **draw conclusions** based on observations made while **using a model**. From your observations of a model landfill, what conclusions can you draw about using paper trash bags instead of plastic trash bags? Students might conclude that paper bags are better because they decay in landfills and plastic bags don't.

**Investigate Further** In many places, items that are not biodegradable are removed from trash before it is collected. **Predict** how quickly trash in landfills would decay if it were all biodegradable. **Make a model** to test your prediction.

**My prediction:** _____

_____

**My model:** _____

_____

**My results:** _____

_____

Name _____

Date _____

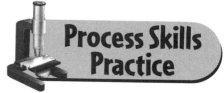

# Using a Model to Draw Conclusions

Using a model involves making or using a representation of a process or structure to better understand how the process works. Examples of models include maps, diagrams, three-dimensional representations, and computer simulations.

## Think About Using a Model to Draw Conclusions

The table below is a simple model showing how many plastic bags Mark would save in a year by using the same bag to carry things from the store instead of getting a new bag two times a week. Each cell lists a month and the number of bags Mark will save by the end of that month if he starts carrying a bag on January 1. Study the model, and answer the questions to draw a conclusion.

| January: | 8 | April: | 34 | July: | 60 | October: | 86 |
| February: | 16 | May: | 42 | August: | 68 | November: | 94 |
| March: | 24 | June: | 50 | September: | 76 | December: | 104 |

1. How many bags would Mark save in a year? _____

   How did the model help you reach that conclusion? _____

   _____

2. Suppose three of Mark's friends think he has a good idea and decide to carry their own bags. These friends buy things about as often as Mark does. Use multiplication to figure out how many bags Mark and his three friends would

   save in a year. _____

3. Another friend decided to follow Mark's example, but half the time he forgot to take his bag to the store. About how many bags would this friend save?

   _____

4. From this mathematical model, draw a conclusion about reusing plastic bags.

   Use the information to argue for or against Mark's practice. _____

   _____

   _____

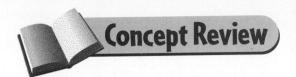

# How Can People Treat Ecosystems More Wisely?

## Lesson Concept

People can treat ecosystems more wisely by reducing pollution, protecting ecosystems, and conserving resources.

## Vocabulary

**conserving** (B104)    **reduce** (B104)    **reuse** (B105)    **recycle** (B105)

**Listed below are several things Carla does to treat ecosystems wisely. After each behavior, tell what resource she is reducing the use of, reusing, or recycling. Some behaviors may accomplish more than one of these goals.**

1. Carla rides her bike to the library instead of riding in a car.
   reduces use of oil and reduces air pollution from auto emissions

2. Instead of buying a new CD, Carla asks Bob if she can borrow his CD.
   reduces use of energy and resources to manufacture, package, and sell the CD

3. Carla's neighbor, Ms. Esposito, has a yard sale to sell used books, CDs, clothes, and other items. Carla buys a used chair to put in her living room.
   reuses items that would be discarded; reduces use of energy and resources to manufacture, package, and sell items; reduces items being thrown away

4. Instead of turning the thermostat to a higher setting, Carla puts on a sweater and a pair of thick socks to keep warm in the winter. reduces use of oil, electricity, or gas to heat buildings

5. Carla needs notebook filler paper for class. She buys paper made from postconsumer waste paper. reduces number of trees that must be cut to make new paper products; recycles a resource to make a new product

6. Carla buys organically grown oranges from the farmers' market to make marmalade. reduces use of pesticides and fertilizers, which protects soil resources and food webs

Name _____

Date _____

# How Waste Water Can Be Cleaned

## Materials

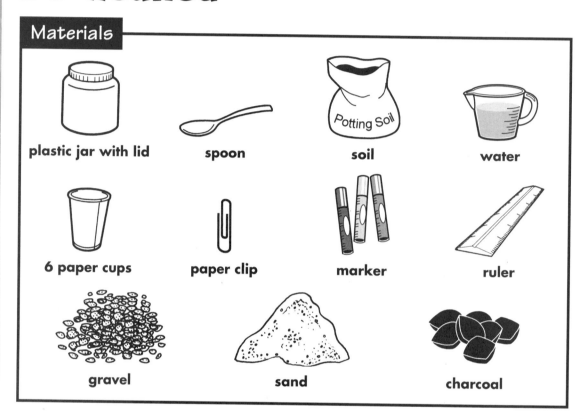

plastic jar with lid  |  spoon  |  soil  |  water

6 paper cups  |  paper clip  |  marker  |  ruler

gravel  |  sand  |  charcoal

## Activity Procedure

**1** Put several spoonfuls of soil in the jar. Then fill the jar with water and put the lid on.

**2** Shake the jar for 15 sec. Then put the jar aside for about 5 min. A process called *sedimentation* is taking place in the jar. It is the first step in waste-water treatment. **Observe** the water in the jar. **Record** your observations.

My observations: _____

_____

**3** Unbend the paper clip. Use it to punch 10 small holes each in the bottoms of 3 paper cups. Using the marker, label the cups *A*, *B*, and *C*.

**4** Using the spoon, put a 2.5-cm layer of gravel in Cup A. Put a 2.5-cm layer of sand and then a 2.5-cm layer of gravel in Cup B. Put a 2.5-cm layer of charcoal, and then a 2.5-cm layer of sand, and finally a 2.5-cm layer of gravel in Cup C.

**5** Put each cup with holes inside a cup without holes. Label the outer cups *A*, *B*, and *C* to match the inner cups. Then carefully pour equal amounts of water from the jar into each set of cups. Try not to shake the jar as you pour. A process called *filtering* is taking place in the cups. It is the second step in waste-water treatment.

**6** Separate each set of cups, allowing all the water to drain into the outer cups. **Observe** the water in the outer cups. **Record** your observations.

**My observations:** _____

_____

## Draw Conclusions

**1.** What did you **observe** happening during sedimentation?

Large particles of soil settled to the bottom of the jar.

**2.** What combination of materials did the best job of filtering the water?

the combination of charcoal, sand, and gravel

**3.** What materials do you **infer** might not be filtered out of waste water?

Answers may include harmful organisms and materials dissolved in water, such as salt or poisonous chemicals.

**4.** **Scientists at Work** Scientists must **identify and control variables** when they **experiment**. In a real waste-water treatment plant, what variables might affect the filtering process? Possible answers: The water might contain materials that require different filtering materials; each step in the filtering process may require more materials; the filtering process may take more time.

**Investigate Further** **Plan and conduct a simple investigation**, using water that is "polluted" with food coloring. Decide what equipment you will need. Test several different kinds of filters.

**My design:** _____

_____

**My observations:** _____

_____

**My results:** _____

_____

# Experiment

When you experiment, you design procedures for gathering data. An experiment tests a hypothesis under conditions in which variables are controlled or manipulated.

## Think About Experimenting

Experiments must be designed carefully so the people running the experiment will know the meaning of the experiment's outcome. Everything that happens in an experiment can affect the outcome. Something the experimenter doesn't notice—like a 2 degree difference in temperature—could have an impact on what happens. That's why experiments must be repeated over and over, with the same results, before experimenters have proved anything. The first step, however, is to design an experiment to test the thing about which the experimenter wants to learn.

**Read the problem that follows, and then design an experiment that will help you find the solution to the problem.**

Rachael plants native bushes and flowers in her yard to attract insects, birds, and other creatures native to her ecosystem. She doesn't use pesticides in her garden. One year, however, she notices small black bugs on a berry bush. She has read about people using soap or garlic on plants to get rid of pests, but she doesn't know how much to use or which would be more effective. She has five bushes of this type, in three different sunny locations in her yard. Design an experiment for

Rachael that would let her test these remedies. _____

_____

_____

_____

_____

_____

_____

_____

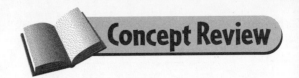

Concept Review

# How Can People Help Restore Damaged Ecosystems?

## Lesson Concept

People can help restore damaged ecosystems by rebuilding them.

## Vocabulary

**reclamation** (B110)          **wetlands** (B111)

Fill in the chart below to describe some of the typical problems found in damaged ecosystems and the solutions people have used.

| Ecosystem | Problems | Solutions |
|---|---|---|
| River | high levels of poisons, like PCBs, in the bodies of fish; other forms of pollution | require treatment of waste water before it is dumped in the river |
| Wetlands | wetlands drained and used for farming or other types of development | rebuild wetlands and protect remaining wetlands |
| Backyard | pollution from fertilizers and pesticides gets into groundwater and also kills animals | plant native grasses, flowers, and bushes that require smaller amounts of water, fertilizers, and pesticides |

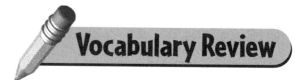
# Recognize Vocabulary

| | | | |
|---|---|---|---|
| succession | pioneer plants | climax community | pollution |
| acid rain | conserving | reduce | reuse |
| recycle | reclamation | wetlands | |

**Fill in the blanks below with the vocabulary terms above to complete the paragraphs about protecting ecosystems.**

Even if most of the plants in an ecosystem are destroyed, hardy

_____ will return and begin to grow, building up the soil
and attracting animals. Over time, through natural _____,
the area will change. The last stage of these slow changes occurs when

a _____ is achieved. If no disasters occur, this
ecosystem will remain unchanged for thousands of years. Unfortunately,

_____ from human activities like manufacturing can
kill organisms and break food chains. Activities like manufacturing, generating
electricity, and operating motor vehicles produce gases that mix with water vapor

in the atmosphere and fall back to Earth as _____.
We can all work to protect ecosystems by buying fewer things and using less

energy. Instead of throwing things away, _____ them a
second or third time. Do you really need a fresh plastic bag every time
you buy something? If you don't need a bag when you buy something, don't get

one. If everyone did this, we would _____ the number
of plastic bags we throw away. A lot of towns and cities encourage people to

_____ newspapers, glass, and plastics.
It's not hard to think of things that individuals and communities

can do if they care about _____ resources.
There are many inspiring stories about people who work together on

_____ projects to restore damaged ecosystems.
If everybody did just a little, it would help protect our ecosystems and
preserve our resources.

# Chapter 1 • Graphic Organizer for Chapter Concepts

## Changes to Earth's Surface

### LESSON 1
### SURFACE PROCESSES THAT CHANGE LANDFORMS

1. weathering _____
2. erosion _____
3. deposition _____

### LESSON 2
### PROCESSES THAT BEGIN IN EARTH'S INTERIOR

1. mountain building _____
2. volcanoes _____
3. earthquakes _____

### LESSON 3
### STAGES IN CONTINENTAL DRIFT

1. Pangea _____
2. Gondwana-Laurasia _____
3. present Earth _____

# How Water Changes Earth's Surface

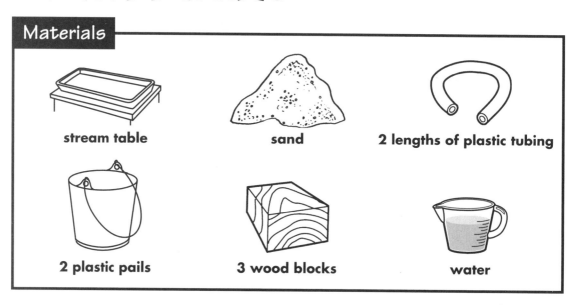

stream table          sand          2 lengths of plastic tubing

2 plastic pails       3 wood blocks          water

## Activity Procedure

1. Place the stream table on a classroom table. Make sure the front end of the stream table is even with the edge of the table. Put the stream-table support under the back end of the stream table.

2. Fill the stream table with sand.

3. Using two fingers, make a path, or channel, down the middle of the sand.

4. Connect one end of one length of tubing to the front of the stream table. Let the other end of the tubing hang over the edge of the table. Place an empty pail on the floor under the hanging end of the tubing.

5. Place the other pail on two wood blocks near the raised end of the stream-table channel. Fill this pail $\frac{3}{4}$ full of water.

6. Put the second length of tubing into the pail, and fill it with water.

7. Start the water flowing through the tube from the pail to the stream table by lowering one end of the filled tube.

8. **Observe** any changes the water makes to the sand in the stream table. **Record** your observations.

9. Place the third wood block on top of the support under the stream table. Repeat Steps 7 and 8.

Name _____

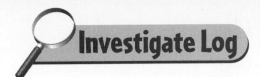
## Draw Conclusions

**1.** In which setup was the speed of the water greater? <u>the second setup</u>

_____

**2.** In which setup did you **observe** greater movement of sand from the channel?

the second setup
_____

**3. Scientists at Work** Scientists learn by **observing**. What did you learn about the way water can change the land by observing the channel in the stream table?

Flowing water moves soil and makes stream channels wider.
_____

Water that flows faster digs deeper and can remove more soil.
_____

**Investigate Further  Hypothesize** what would happen if you replaced the sand with soil. **Experiment** to test your hypothesis.

_____

_____

_____

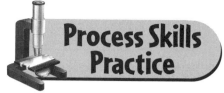

# Observe

You observe by using your senses to see, hear, smell, and feel the world around you.

## Think About Observing

Think about the things you see every day that may have been changed by moving water or ice. You may observe the dirt and gravel that pile up at the end of the street or the holes in the street that have to be repaired every year. What kinds of changes have you seen? Fill in the chart below with your observations and the possible causes for them. Two examples have been provided.

| Observation | Possible Cause |
|---|---|
| 1. Roots of plants growing on the side of a drainage ditch have been exposed. | 1. Rushing water during heavy rain has washed soil away from the roots. |
| 2. Bits of gravel have piled up under the downspout that comes from the roof. | 2. Rainwater has washed bits of gravel off the roof shingles. |
| 3. | 3. |
| 4. | 4. |
| 5. | 5. |
| 6. | 6. |

**1.** What do you think would happen if rain continued to wash away the soil in Observation 1 on the chart? _____

_____

_____

**2.** What do you think would happen to the roof in Observation 2?

_____

**3.** How do you think the scenes you observed will change over the passing of many years? _____

_____

_____

**Use with page C5.**

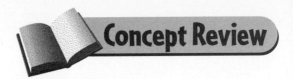

# What Processes Change Landforms?

## Lesson Concept

The action of water, wind, ice, and gravity break down Earth's crust and change landforms.

## Vocabulary

| | | |
|---|---|---|
| **landforms** (C6) | **weathering** (C7) | **erosion** (C7) |
| **deposition** (C7) | **mass movement** (C9) | |

**Answer each question with one or more complete sentences.**

**1.** Most of the time, changes to landforms are slow. What are some examples of very fast changes? Possible answers include a hurricane washing away a beach, a volcano erupting and enlarging an island, or a mudslide filling in part of a lake.

**2.** What are two landforms that can be caused by glaciers? Terminal moraines and U-shaped valleys can be caused by glaciers.

**3.** Why has wind erosion shaped so many landforms in the American Southwest? There is very little plant life to hold the soil in place, so the dry soil is picked up and blown against the rocky landforms by the wind.

**4.** Name three kinds of mass movement. Three kinds of mass movement are mudslides, landslides, and creep.

**5.** How is a river delta formed? Sediments are picked up and carried away by the river. When the river slows down as it empties into the ocean, it deposits the sediments. They build up and eventually form a delta.

**Investigate Log**

# Journey to the Center of Earth

## Materials

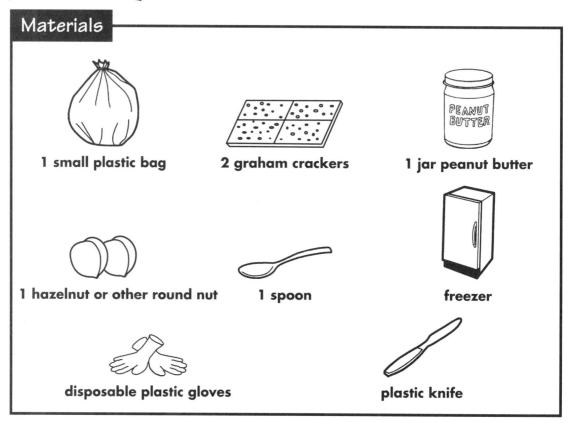

**1 small plastic bag**  **2 graham crackers**  **1 jar peanut butter**

**1 hazelnut or other round nut**  **1 spoon**  **freezer**

**disposable plastic gloves**  **plastic knife**

## Activity Procedure

1. Put the graham crackers in the plastic bag. Close the bag and use your hands to crush the crackers into crumbs. Then set the bag aside.

2. Put on the plastic gloves. Use the spoon to scoop a glob of peanut butter from the jar and put it in your gloved hand. Place the nut in the center of the peanut butter. Cover the nut with more peanut butter until there is about 2.5 cm of peanut butter all around the nut. Using both hands, roll the glob of peanut butter with the nut at its center into a ball.

3. Open the bag of crushed graham crackers, and roll the peanut-butter ball in the graham cracker crumbs until the outside of the ball is completely coated.

4. Put the ball in the freezer for about 15 minutes. Remove the ball and cut into your model with the plastic knife. **Observe** the layers inside. You might want to take a photograph of your model for later review.

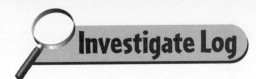
## Draw Conclusions

1. The peanut-butter ball is a model of Earth's layers. How many layers does Earth have in this model? _three_____

2. Which layer of Earth do the crushed graham crackers represent? Why do you think your model has a thick layer of peanut butter but a thin layer of graham cracker crumbs? _the crust; the mantle (peanut butter) is thicker than the crust_

   _____

   _____

3. **Scientists at Work** Scientists can see and understand complex structures better by **making models** of them. What does the model show about Earth's layers? What doesn't the model show about Earth's layers? _It shows how many_ _layers Earth has, the shapes of the layers, and the relative thickness of the_ _layers. The model does not show what Earth's layers are made of._

   _____

**Investigate Further** Some geologists, scientists who study the Earth, say that Earth's center is divided into a soft outer part and a hard inner part. How could you **make a model** to show this? _____

_____

_____

_____

# Make and Use Models

Sometimes making a model can give you a better understanding of a process. This is especially so when you are trying to understand an Earth process, which takes millions of years to occur.

### Think About Making and Using Models

Suppose you are using biscuit dough to model the movement of Earth's surface. First you would roll the dough flat and cut two blocks out of it. Those blocks would model two opposing plates of Earth's crust. Suppose you put them together as shown and push them against one another. Then think of trying to slide them past one another.

1. What is the dough modeling when the two blocks are pushed together?

_____

_____

2. What do you think happens when you try to slide the blocks of dough past one another? What do you think this models? _____

_____

_____

_____

3. You have seen how this model is similar to Earth's surface, or crust. How is this model different? _____

_____

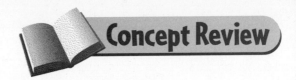

# What Causes Mountains, Volcanoes, and Earthquakes?

## Lesson Concept

Earth has three layers. The outer layer, or crust, is broken into tectonic plates. The movement of the plates results in mountains, volcanoes, and earthquakes.

## Vocabulary

| | | | |
|---|---|---|---|
| **crust** (C14) | **mantle** (C14) | **core** (C14) | **plate** (C15) |
| **magma** (C16) | **volcano** (C16) | **earthquake** (C18) | **fault** (C18) |

**Choose from the vocabulary list, and add the missing words to the paragraph below. Use each vocabulary term only once.**

The _____ core _____ is Earth's center and its hottest layer. It is divided into two parts. The outer section is molten rock. Great pressure keeps the inner section solid. The middle layer of Earth is called

the _____ mantle _____. It is made of hot, soft rock called

_____ magma _____. This hot, soft rock sometimes reaches

Earth's upper layer through openings called _____ volcanoes _____.
The hot, soft rock is called lava when it flows on Earth's surface. The outermost

layer of Earth is called the _____ crust _____. It is made of many

_____ plates _____ that float on the soft rock below them. When these pieces of Earth's surface crash together or scrape against one another,

the release of energy causes an _____ earthquake _____. The places where pieces of Earth's crust move can bend or break. These breaks can become

_____ faults _____.

# Movement of the Continents

## Materials

**3 copies of a world map**

**scissors**

**globe or world map**

**glue**

**3 sheets of construction paper**

## Activity Procedure

**1** Cut out the continents from one copy of the world map.

**2** Arrange the continents into one large "supercontinent" on a sheet of construction paper. As you would with a jigsaw puzzle, arrange them so their edges fit together as closely as possible.

**3** Label the pieces with the names of their present continents, and glue them onto the paper.

**4** Use a globe or world map to locate the following mountains: Cascades, Andes, Atlas, Himalayas, Alps. Then draw these mountains on the supercontinent.

**5** Use your textbook to locate volcanoes and places where earthquakes have occurred. Put a *V* in places where you know there are volcanoes, such as the Cascades. Put an *E* in places where you know that earthquakes have occurred, such as western North America.

**6** Repeat Steps 1–5 with the second copy of the world map, but before gluing the continents to the construction paper, separate them by about 2.5 cm. That is, leave about 2.5 cm of space between North America and Eurasia, between South America and Africa, and so on.

**7** Glue the third world map copy onto a sheet of construction paper. Then place the three versions of the world map in order from the oldest to the youngest.

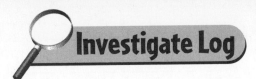
## Draw Conclusions

**1.** Where do the continents fit together the best? Possible answers: the western
edge of Africa and the eastern edge of South America; the bulge of Africa
and the curve of the eastern coast of North America

_____

**2.** Where are most of the mountains, volcanoes, and earthquake sites in relation
to the present continents? Why do you think they are there?
Most are at the edges of the present continents, near plate boundaries.

_____

**3. Scientists at Work** Scientists use **models**, such as maps, to better understand
complex structures and processes. How did your models of Earth's continents
help you **draw conclusions** about Earth's past? The continents were once
joined and have slowly moved to their present locations.

What limitations did your models have? The map doesn't show how the
continents moved or how fast they moved.

**Investigate Further  Hypothesize** about the fact that the continents do not fit
together exactly. Then **plan and conduct a simple investigation** to test your

hypothesis. _____

_____

_____

_____

# Make a Model

Making a model can help you understand an object or a process. You use models to find out about things all the time. When you use a map, you are using a model of a specific geographic area.

## Think About Making a Model

In the space below, draw a map that someone could use to get from your house to your school. Show special landmarks, such as large buildings, trees, or other objects, that a person could use as help in following your map.

_____

**1.** Write a paragraph telling someone how to get from your house to your school.

_____
_____
_____
_____

**2.** Do you think someone could use your map and get from your house to school without reading the paragraph you wrote? _____

_____
_____

**3.** Is your map a good model of the process of getting from your house to school? Why or why not? _____

_____

**4.** What could you do to make your map more accurate? _____

_____
_____

Name _____

Date _____

# How Has Earth's Surface Changed?

## Lesson Concept

Earth's surface features have changed over millions of years.
Fossils help scientists learn about plants and animals of the past.

## Vocabulary

**continental drift** (C22)     **Pangea** (C22)     **fossils** (C23)

**Review the concepts in Lesson 3 by answering the following riddles.**

**1.** At my deepest point, I'm a mile-deep slice into Earth's history—and a very

popular tourist attraction. What am I? _Grand Canyon_____

**2.** There are continents, and then there is . . . SUPERCONTINENT! I don't wear a
cape, but I once included all the land on Earth. What am I?

_Pangea_____

**3.** We were left behind a long time ago, but today we can tell you a lot about

Earth's history. What are we? _fossils_____

**4.** In observing rock layers, I am usually found on the bottom. What am I?

_the oldest layer_____

**5.** Scientists have found fossils on the tops of mountains. What do they infer?

_that the area was once covered by water_____

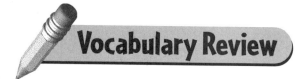
# Recognize Vocabulary

Listed below are the vocabulary terms from this chapter. Match the terms in Column A with the definitions in Column B by writing the letter of the correct definition in the space next to the term.

**Column A**

_____ **1.** landform

_____ **2.** weathering

_____ **3.** erosion

_____ **4.** deposition

_____ **5.** mass movement

_____ **6.** crust

_____ **7.** mantle

_____ **8.** core

_____ **9.** plate

_____ **10.** magma

_____ **11.** volcano

_____ **12.** earthquake

_____ **13.** fault

_____ **14.** continental drift

_____ **15.** Pangea

_____ **16.** fossils

**Column B**

**A** the downhill movement of rock and soil because of gravity

**B** hot, soft rock from Earth's lower mantle

**C** Earth's hottest layer; the center layer of Earth

**D** the process of breaking rock into soil, sand, or other tiny pieces

**E** a shaking of the ground caused by the sudden release of energy in Earth's crust

**F** an opening in Earth's crust through which lava flows

**G** the layer of rock beneath Earth's crust

**H** the process of dropping, or depositing, sediment in a new location

**I** the theory of how Earth's continents move over its surface

**J** the process of moving sediment from one place to another

**K** According to theory, this was a "supercontinent" that contained all of Earth's land about 225 million years ago.

**L** a rigid block of crust and upper mantle

**M** the remains or traces of past life found in Earth's crust

**N** the outer layer of Earth made of solid rock

**O** a physical feature of Earth's surface

**P** a place where pieces of Earth's crust move

Name _____  Date _____

# Chapter 2 • Graphic Organizer for Chapter Concepts

## Renewable and Nonrenewable Resources

# Properties of Minerals

## Materials

6 mineral samples
(talc, pyrite, quartz, fluorite,
magnetite, graphite)

tile

magnet

## Activity Procedure

**1** Use the following chart.

| Mineral | Hardness | Shine | Streak | Magnetic |
|---------|----------|-------|--------|----------|
| talc | | | | |
| pyrite | | | | |
| quartz | | | | |
| fluorite | | | | |
| magnetite | | | | |
| graphite | | | | |

**2** **Observe** each mineral. **Predict** which one will be the hardest. Then rub the
minerals against each other to test their hardness. A harder mineral will
scratch a softer one. Under *Hardness* on the chart, write a number from 1 to
6 for the hardness of each mineral. Use 1 for the softest mineral. Use 6 for
the hardest mineral.

**3** **Observe** each mineral, and decide whether or not it is shiny. Write *yes* next
to the name of the mineral if it is shiny. Write *no* if it is not.

Name _____

④ Now **predict** the color of the streak
each mineral will make. A streak is the colored line a mineral makes when it
is rubbed on a tile. Then rub each mineral on the tile. If the mineral makes a
streak, write the color of the streak next to the mineral's name. Write *none* if
the mineral does not make a streak.

⑤ Finally, **predict** which minerals will be attracted to a magnet. Test each
mineral with a magnet. Write *yes* next to the names of minerals that stick
to the magnet. Write *no* next to the names of those that do not.

## Draw Conclusions

1. Which mineral is the softest? **Compare** your test results with your predictions.
   Minerals in order from softest to hardest are talc, graphite, fluorite, pyrite,
   magnetite, quartz.

   _____

2. Which minerals make streaks? **Compare** your test results with your color
   predictions. Mineral streaks: pyrite—green/black; magnetite—black;
   fluorite—white; graphite—gray/black; the others do not make a streak.

   _____

3. Which minerals are magnetic? **Compare** your test results with your
   predictions. magnetite, pyrite

   _____

4. **Scientists at Work** Scientists often **predict** what might happen. How did
   careful observations of the mineral samples help you make better predictions
   about their properties? Answers should include the idea that careful
   observations make predictions more likely to be correct.

   _____

**Investigate Further** Use the information you gathered on each mineral's

properties to **infer** its uses. _____

_____

_____

_____

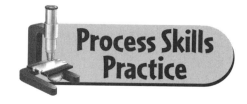

## Process Skills Practice

# Predict

One way to check your understanding of something is to predict an outcome, and then see how closely your prediction matches the actual outcome. The first step is to interpret the data you have collected.

### Think About Predicting

In 1955 each farm worker in the United States produced enough food to feed 20 people. By 1960 farming methods had improved, and one worker could supply 25 people. In 1965 that number became 40 people. In 1970 it was 45 people. In 1975 it increased to 60 people. In 1980 one farm worker could supply 75 people. Graph this data in the grid to the right to show how production increased with time. Then use the graph to help you predict.

1. How many people do you think were supplied by one farm worker in 1990?

_____

_____

2. Will a graph like this help you predict far into the future? Why or why not?

_____

_____

_____

**Concept Review**

# What Are Natural Resources?

## Lesson Concept

Natural resources are useful materials that people take from Earth.
Some resources are renewable or reusable. Others are nonrenewable.
Once nonrenewable resources are used, they cannot be replaced.

## Vocabulary

**natural resource** (C36)          **nonrenewable resource** (C36)

**renewable resource** (C38)        **reusable resource** (C38)

### Which kind of resources are these?

Next to each resource listed below, write whether the resource is renewable,
reusable, or nonrenewable. Explain your answer.

| Resource | Type and Explanation |
|---|---|
| **1.** water | Reusable; the water cycle allows Earth's water supply to be used over and over again. |
| **2.** oil | Nonrenewable; oil is a fossil fuel that took millions of years to form. Once it is used up, there is no more. |
| **3.** wood | Renewable; the trees will grow back again. |
| **4.** soil | Renewable; when plants and animals decay, minerals and other nutrients are returned to the soil. |
| **5.** gasoline | Nonrenewable; gasoline comes from oil, which is a fossil fuel. |

# What Kinds of Rocks Store Petroleum?

## Materials

limestone

shale

mineral oil

sandstone

paper plates

dropper

clock

## Activity Procedure

1 Place the rock samples on separate paper plates. **Observe** each rock. **Predict** which will be the best storage rock.

2 Fill the dropper with mineral oil. Put 5 drops of oil on the limestone sample.

3 **Observe** and **record** the time it takes for the 5 drops of oil to soak into the limestone.

4 Continue adding oil, counting the drops, until the limestone will hold no more oil. **Record** the number of drops it takes.

5 Repeat Steps 2–4 with the other rock samples.

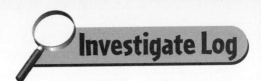
## Draw Conclusions

**1.** Which rock soaked up the oil the fastest? What was the time?

sandstone; times will vary

_____

**2.** Which rock soaked up the most oil? What was the number of drops?

sandstone; number of drops will vary

_____

**3.** Which rock is the best storage rock? Explain. sandstone; it holds the most oil

_____

**4. Scientists at Work** Scientists often **use numbers** to **compare** things. How did you use numbers to compare the oil-storing ability of the rocks?

by comparing the number of drops of oil that the different rocks hold

_____

**Investigate Further** How could you determine which of the rocks is a source rock for petroleum? **Plan a simple investigation** to answer this question. Then decide what equipment you would need to carry out this investigation. _____

_____

_____

_____

# Use Numbers and Compare

Numbers give you a way to estimate things. They allow you to count, order, or compare information.

## Think About Using Numbers and Comparing

The table below on the left shows how many quadrillion Btus (a way of measuring energy) were used in 1995 by the countries listed. Find the largest number in the "Btus" column. Put that number at the top of the Btus column in the table on the right. Next to that number, write the name of the country that used that amount of energy. Complete the table, ordering the numbers from largest to smallest.

| Country | Btus |
|---|---|
| Germany | 13.71 |
| United Kingdom | 9.85 |
| China | 35.67 |
| Italy | 7.42 |
| Russia | 26.75 |
| Canada | 11.72 |
| United States | 90.94 |
| Japan | 21.42 |
| France | 9.43 |
| India | 10.50 |

| Btus | Country |
|---|---|
|  |  |
|  |  |
|  |  |
|  |  |
|  |  |
|  |  |
|  |  |
|  |  |
|  |  |
|  |  |

1. What is the total energy used by the five European countries listed? What is the total energy used by the three Asian countries? How do these figures compare?

   _____

   _____

2. What did you learn from adding and comparing the numbers showing European and Asian energy use? _____

   _____

   _____

Name _____

Date _____

# How Do Fossil Fuels Form?

## Lesson Concept

Fossil fuels form over millions of years from the decayed remains of organisms. Coal forms in four stages, first forming peat, then lignite, then bitumen, and finally anthracite.

## Vocabulary

**peat** (C44)        **lignite** (C44)        **bitumen** (C45)

**anthracite** (C45)        **natural gas** (C46)        **fossil fuels** (C42)

Write the letter of the definition in Column B next to the word it defines in Column A.

**Column A**

___N___ 70 percent

___L___ anthracite

___G___ the sun

___J___ sedimentary

___C___ petroleum

___H___ bitumen

___M___ swamps

___B___ coal

___K___ seams

___A___ fossil fuels

___F___ natural gas

___E___ lignite

___D___ peat

___I___ petrochemicals

**Column B**

**A** coal, natural gas, and petroleum

**B** the most common fossil fuel

**C** fossil fuel that formed when microorganisms died and fell to the bottoms of ancient seas

**D** first stage of coal formation

**E** soft, brown rock that forms as layers of sand and mud cover peat

**F** mostly methane, usually found with petroleum

**G** source of the energy in fossil fuels

**H** third stage of coal formation

**I** chemicals made from petroleum

**J** kind of rock in which fossil fuels are usually found

**K** layers of coal

**L** fourth stage of coal formation

**M** places where peat can be found

**N** amount of carbon in lignite

**Use with page C47.**

# How People Use Natural Resources

## Materials

small bowl of paper clips

3 generation cards
(parents, children, grandchildren)

## Activity Procedure

1. Work in a group of three. Place your group's generation cards face down on a table. The bowl of paper clips stands for Earth's supply of a certain resource, such as iron.

2. Each person in the group now takes a generation card. Hold up your card so the other people in your group can see it. The card tells you your generation. It also tells you how many people are in your generation.

3. Each generation will now get paper clips from the bowl. The person from the parents' generation goes first. He or she takes five clips from the bowl for each person in his or her generation.

4. Next, the person from the children's generation takes five clips for each person in his or her generation.

5. Finally, the person from the grandchildren's generation takes five clips for each person in his or her generation.

Name _____

## Draw Conclusions

**1.** Did everyone get the same number of clips? no _____

**2.** Where did a problem occur? Grandchildren did not get their full share. _____

_____

**3.** What could be done to avoid the problem? Reduce the number of clips _____

for each person in the parents' and children's generations.

**4. Scientists at Work** Scientists **hypothesize** what the results of an investigation might be. Hypothesize what will happen if each person from a generation gets only three or four clips, instead of five. There would be enough clips _____

for the grandchildren if each person gets three clips, but not if each

person gets four.

_____

**Investigate Further** With the members of your group, list the products people use that are made from a natural resource, such as a certain metal. Describe several things people could do to make sure that in the future there will be enough of this resource. Then **plan and conduct a simple investigation** using technology to simulate your plan. _____

_____

_____

_____

# Hypothesize

A hypothesis is an educated "guess" about how one thing will be affected by another thing. A hypothesis is based on observation and prior knowledge. It can be tested in an experiment and changed depending on the result of the experiment.

## Think About Hypothesizing

In some places trucks pick up newspapers, glass, cans, and plastics to be recycled. In other places people must take these items to a recycling center. In some states people get money back when they recycle certain types of glass or plastic bottles. Some towns put up billboards reminding people to recycle. What makes people more likely to recycle?

1. Think about the following hypothesis: If you pay people to recycle, then more people will recycle. How could you test this hypothesis?

   _____

   _____

2. What results would support the hypothesis? _____

   _____

   _____

   _____

3. Some people hypothesize that if you make recycling easier for people, then they will recycle. How can you test this hypothesis? _____

   _____

   _____

4. Some people hypothesize that if you educate people about the importance of recycling, then they will recycle. How can you test this hypothesis? _____

   _____

   _____

5. Hypothesize which of the three methods given above would be most effective in getting people to recycle. Support your hypothesis. _____

   _____

   _____

# How Are Natural Resources Conserved?

## Lesson Concept

Earth has a limited supply of natural resources that must be conserved so that they will last as long as possible.

## Vocabulary

**recycling** (C52)

One way to conserve resources is to reduce the amounts that are used. Another way is to reuse things. Many things that can't be reused can be recycled. Think of things you could do to conserve resources by **reducing**, **reusing**, or **recycling**. Next to each resource below, describe what you could do to conserve that resource.

### Reduce

1. **Gasoline** Possible answers include riding your bike instead of having someone drive you somewhere, planning your errands so you could get them all done in one trip, or staying home.

2. **Coal (Electricity)** Possible answers include turning off lights when you leave a room; hanging your gym socks on a drying rack instead of putting them in the dryer; or turning off the television, computer, or game and doing something that doesn't require electricity.

### Reuse

3. **Plastics** Possible answers include using a washable container for a sandwich instead of a plastic bag, carrying bags to the grocery so you don't need to use new ones, and using a refillable ballpoint pen instead of a disposable one.

### Recycle

4. **Trees (Paper)** Possible answers include putting papers in recycling bins instead of trash cans and buying items made from recycled paper.

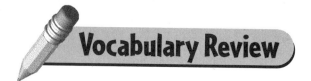
# Recognize Vocabulary

Review the vocabulary terms for Chapter 2 by completing this word puzzle.

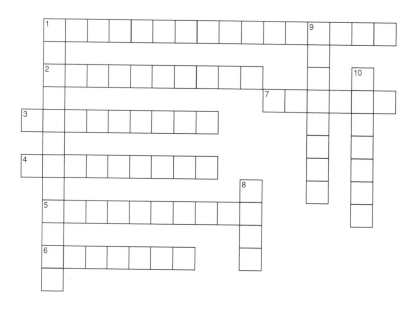

## Across

**1.** Minerals and other useful materials that are taken from Earth (2 words)

**2.** A fossil fuel consisting mostly of methane (2 words)

**3.** A resource that's replaced as it is used is called a _____ resource.

**4.** The process of taking back the resource in a product

**5.** A very hard, black rock that is the most valuable form of coal

**6.** This is formed when pressure squeezes moisture out of peat

**7.** Burned to heat homes and produce electricity, _____ fuels are formed from decayed organisms in Earth.

## Down

**1.** A resource that cannot be replaced is called a _____ resource.

**8.** A soft, brown material made up of partially decayed plants

**9.** A resource that can be used more than once is called a _____ resource.

**10.** The most common type of coal mined and used today

# Chapter 3 • Graphic Organizer for Chapter Concepts

## Weather and Climate

### LESSON 1
### WEATHER FACTORS

**Atmosphere**

1. troposphere _____

2. stratosphere _____

**Air Pressure**

1. low pressure—warmer air _____

2. high pressure—cooler air _____

**Humidity**

**Precipitation**

**Water Cycle**

evaporation ⟶
condensation ⟶

**Clouds**

1. cirrus _____

2. cumulus _____

3. stratus _____

4. cumulonimbus _____

### LESSON 2
### WIND

**Caused by Sun's Uneven Heating of Earth**

1. some energy absorbed by atmosphere _____

2. some energy reflected back by Earth _____

3. some energy absorbed by Earth _____

**Types of Wind**

1. local winds _____

2. prevailing winds _____

### LESSON 3
### CLIMATE

**Average of All Weather Over Time**

**Climate Zones**

1. polar _____

2. tropical _____

3. temperate _____

4. mountain _____

5. desert _____

**Climate Changes**

1. El Niño _____

2. greenhouse effect _____

3. global warming _____

# Measuring Weather Conditions

## Materials

weather station

## Activity Procedure

**1** Use the Weather Station Daily Record chart below to **record** the date, the time, the temperature, the amount of rain or snow, the wind direction and speed, and the cloud conditions each day for five days. Try to **record** the weather conditions at the same time each day.

**2** Place the weather station in a shady spot, 1 m above the ground. **Record** the temperature.

**3** Be sure the rain gauge will not collect runoff from any buildings or trees. **Record** the amount of rain or snow (if any).

**4** Be sure the wind vane is located where wind from any direction will reach it. **Record** the wind direction and speed. Winds are labeled with the direction from which they blow.

| Weather Station Daily Record | | | | | |
|---|---|---|---|---|---|
| Date | | | | | |
| Time | | | | | |
| Temperature | | | | | |
| Rainfall or snowfall | | | | | |
| Wind direction and speed | | | | | |
| Cloud condition | | | | | |

**Investigate Log**

**5** Describe and **record** the cloud conditions by noting how much of the sky is covered by clouds. Draw a circle and shade in the part of the circle that equals the amount of sky covered with clouds.

**6** Use the temperature data to make a line graph showing how the temperature changes from day to day.

## Draw Conclusions

**1.** Use your Weather Station Daily Record to **compare** the weather conditions on two different days. Which conditions were about the same? Which conditions changed the most? Students might note differences in temperature, amount of rain or snow, wind direction and speed, and cloud conditions.

**2.** From the **data** you **gathered** in this activity, how might scientists use weather data to **predict** the weather? Possible answer: Scientists might look for trends in weather conditions and use the data to predict the weather.

**3. Scientists at Work** Scientists learn about the weather by **measuring** weather conditions and **gathering data**. What did you learn by measuring the amount of rain your area received during the week of your observations? Students should realize that the total amount of rain an area receives may come from only one or two storms.

**Investigate Further** Find a newspaper weather page, and note the temperatures in various cities throughout the United States. Why are there different temperatures in different cities? **Plan and conduct a simple investigation** using technology to find out. _____

**Process Skills Practice**

# Measure and Collect Data

Measurements are a kind of observation. You measure when you use a tool, such as a thermometer, a clock, or a ruler.

## Think About Measuring and Collecting Data

When you measure, you are actually comparing. For example, if you measure a rope and find that the rope is 1.5 m long, you are comparing the length of the rope to a standard length. The standard is, in this case, the meter. If you weigh the rope and find that it weighs 20 newtons, you are comparing the rope to a standard weight, the newton. Of course, it's important to use the right measuring unit, too. For example, you wouldn't measure a 5-m rope in kilometers. You would use meters. Think about setting a new standard for measuring lengths as shown below.

**thumb**   **span**   **cubit**

**pace**

1. Which of these units would you use to measure the length of a swimming pool?
   _____

2. Which would you use to measure your height? _____
   _____

3. How many spans equal a cubit? _____
   _____

4. Why do you think no one uses a measuring system like this one?
   _____
   _____
   _____

5. How could you make this measuring system work as a standard?
   _____
   _____

Name _____

Date _____

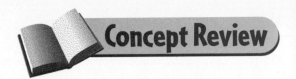

# How Can You Observe and Measure Weather Conditions?

## Lesson Concept

Weather conditions such as temperature, air pressure, humidity, wind speed and direction, and precipitation can be observed and measured.

## Vocabulary

**atmosphere** (C64)   **air pressure** (C65)   **humidity** (C65)

**precipitation** (C65)   **evaporation** (C67)   **condensation** (C67)

**Answer each question with one or more complete sentences.**

1. Where in the atmosphere does most weather occur? Most weather occurs in the troposphere.

2. Why does most weather occur only in one layer of the atmosphere? Most of the water in the atmosphere is in the troposphere. Therefore, that is where the clouds form and weather occurs. Also, there is not enough air above the troposphere.

3. What is the largest source of water for the water cycle? The ocean is the largest source of water for the water cycle.

4. Fog is actually a cloud that is low enough to touch the ground. What kind of cloud is fog? Fog is made of stratus clouds that are near the ground.

5. What are you measuring when you measure air pressure? You are measuring the weight of the atmosphere.

6. Why do people measure atmospheric conditions? When they measure atmospheric conditions, they can predict what the weather will be.

7. If you see cumulus clouds in the sky, what type of weather are you likely to have? Cumulus clouds usually mean fair weather, but they can also produce light rain or snow.

**Use with page C69.**

# The Sun's Energy Heats Unevenly

## Materials

**2 tin cans (lids removed)**

**water**

**dry soil**

**spoon**

**2 thermometers**

## Activity Procedure

1. Fill one can about $\frac{3}{4}$ full of water and the other can about $\frac{3}{4}$ full of soil.

2. Place one thermometer in the can of water and the other in the can of soil. Put the cans in a shady place outside. Wait for 10 minutes, and then **record** the temperatures of the water and the soil.

3. Put both cans in sunlight. **Predict** which of the cans will show the faster rise in temperature. **Record** the temperature of each can every 10 minutes for 30 minutes. In which can does the temperature rise faster? Which material— soil or water—heats up faster?

4. Now put the cans back in the shade. **Predict** in which of the cans the temperature will drop faster. Again **record** the temperature of each can every 10 minutes for 30 minutes. In which can does the temperature drop faster? Which material—soil or water—cools off faster?

5. Make line graphs to show how the temperatures of both materials changed as they heated up and cooled off.

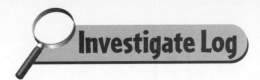

**Investigate Log**

## Draw Conclusions

**1.** How did your results match your predictions? Which material—water or soil—heated up faster? Which cooled off faster? Predictions will vary, but results should show that the can of soil heated up faster and cooled off faster than the can of water.

_____

**2.** From the results you **observed** in this investigation, which would you **predict** heats up faster—oceans or land? Which would you predict cools off faster? Explain. Based on the results students should predict that land heats up faster and cools off faster than oceans.

_____

**3. Scientists at Work** Scientists learn by **predicting** and then testing their predictions. How did you test your predictions about water and soil? The predictions were tested by measuring the temperatures of water and soil as they heated up and cooled off.

_____

**Investigate Further Predict** how fast other materials, such as moist soil, sand, and salt water, heat up and cool off. **Plan and conduct a simple** investigation to test your predictions. _____

_____

_____

_____

_____

# Predict

When you predict, you make a statement about what you think will happen. To make a prediction, you think about what you've observed before. You also think about how to interpret data you have.

## Think About Predicting

Robert wanted to see if he could predict the weather if he knew which way the wind was blowing and whether the barometer was rising or falling. He decided to find out. All through the winter, he kept records of wind direction, air pressure, and the weather that followed his observations. Then he made this chart.

| Wind Direction (From) | Barometer | Weather |
|---|---|---|
| varies | neither rising nor falling | pleasant weather, no changes in temperature |
| south, changing to southeast | falling | wind picks up, rain after a few hours |
| southeast, changing to northeast | falling | windy and colder |
| east, changing to northeast | falling slowly | rain the next day |
| east, changing to northeast | falling rapidly | wind increases, and it snows |
| south, changing to southwest | rising slowly | the skies clear, and the sun comes out |
| southwest, changing to west | rising rapidly | the skies clear, and it gets really cold |

1. Using Robert's chart, what kind of weather would you predict if the wind is from the southwest and the barometer is neither rising nor falling?

   _____

2. Using Robert's chart, what kind of weather would you predict if the barometer is rising and the wind direction has changed from the south to the southwest?

   _____

3. The wind direction has changed from the east to the northeast, and the barometer is falling fast. Using Robert's chart, what kind of weather would you predict?

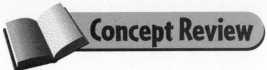

# What Causes Wind?

## Lesson Concept

Changes in air pressure, caused by uneven heating of Earth's surface and the air above it, cause the wind to blow. There are local winds and prevailing winds.

## Vocabulary

| | |
|---|---|
| **local winds** (C73) | **prevailing winds** (C73) |

You know that weather conditions are caused by factors like temperature, humidity, and air pressure. The combinations of these factors form weather systems. A weather system can be a storm, very cold air, or pleasant, sunny weather. Weather systems are moved by prevailing winds from west to east across the United States.

1.  Suppose weather conditions in your area are hot and dry. Do you think local winds are blowing toward the center of the hot area or away from it? Explain. Local winds are probably blowing toward the center of the hot area. As the hot air rises, it forms an area of low pressure. Air moves from areas of higher pressure to lower pressure.

2.  In which general direction is the hot and dry air mass in Question 1 most likely to move? Why? It will most likely move from west to east because of the prevailing winds.

3.  Suppose it is raining today in Ohio and Michigan. What kind of weather would you expect to find in New York state tomorrow? rain

4.  What causes prevailing winds? uneven heating of large parts of the atmosphere and the rotation of Earth

# Local Weather Conditions

**4 metersticks**          **4 weather stations**

## Activity Procedure

**1** Use the table below.

| Local Weather Conditions | | | |
|---|---|---|---|
| **Location** | **Temperature** | **Wind Direction** | **Wind Speed** |
| 1 | | | |
| 2 | | | |
| 3 | | | |
| 4 | | | |

**2** Choose four locations near your school to study. Select different kinds of locations, such as a shady parkway, a sunny playground, a parking lot on the south side of your school, and a ball field on the north side. For the same time on any given day, **predict** whether the temperature, wind direction, and wind speed will be the same or different at the different locations.

**3** At the chosen time, four people should each take a meterstick and a weather station to a different one of the selected locations. Use the meterstick to locate a point 1 m above the ground. **Measure** and **record** the temperature at that point. Use the weather station to determine the wind direction and speed, too. Record the data in your table.

**4** Make a double-bar graph to show the temperatures and wind speeds recorded at all the locations. Write the wind direction at each location on the appropriate wind-speed bar.

Name _____

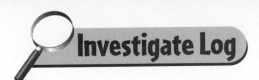 

## Draw Conclusions

**1.** Use your table to **compare** the temperature, wind direction, and wind speed at the different locations. What differences, if any, did you find? What conditions were the same? Answers may vary. Students should note differences in temperature, wind direction, and wind speed for some of the locations.

_____

_____

**2.** Local weather conditions affect the organisms that live in a location. Do you think wind speed or temperature is more likely to affect living organisms? Explain. Answers may vary. Temperature will have a more direct effect, but wind speed could also affect how hot or cold an area is.

_____

_____

**3.** Based on your investigation, how would you define the phrase *local weather conditions*? Possible answer: "weather conditions in a small area"

_____

_____

_____

**4. Scientists at Work** Scientists learn about local weather conditions by **comparing** weather data from different locations. **Draw conclusions** about local weather conditions, based on the locations you studied. Students should realize that many different local weather conditions can exist in a small area.

_____

**Investigate Further** What other factors, in addition to temperature, wind direction, and wind speed might affect local weather conditions? **Hypothesize** about a factor that might affect local weather conditions. Then **plan and conduct a simple investigation** to test your hypothesis. _____

_____

_____

_____

Name _____

Date _____

# Compare and Draw Conclusions

When you compare objects or events, you look for what they have in common. You also look for differences between them.

## Think About Comparing and Drawing Conclusions

Earth's climates can be grouped into five major climate zones. In this activity you can compare three of those climate zones. Use the map and the descriptions of three world climates to answer the questions below.

Polar climates are the world's coldest. Winter temperatures fall below −50°C.

Temperate climates have four seasons a year, with a warm or hot summer and a cool or dry winter. Average daily temperatures range between −3°C in the winter and 18°C in the summer. These areas have an average amount of precipitation.

Tropical climates are found in most of Earth's rain forests and savannas. These areas have an average daily temperature of 27°C and high rainfall.

1. Do you think the climate of Brazil is similar to or different from that of
   Greenland? Explain. _____

   _____

2. Do you think the climate in New Zealand would be very different from the
   climate in New Jersey? _____

   _____

   _____

**Use with page C77.**

Name _____

Date _____

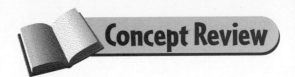

# What Is Climate and How Does It Change?

## Lesson Concept

Climate is the average of all weather conditions through all seasons over a period of time. Earth's climate has changed over time as average temperatures have risen and fallen. Human activities can affect climate.

## Vocabulary

**climate** (C78)    **microclimate** (C78)    **El Niño** (C81)

**greenhouse effect** (C82)    **global warming** (C82)

**Fill in the chart with information from your textbook and answer the questions.**

| Climate Zones | Summer Temp. | Winter Temp. | Precipitation | Where Found? |
|---|---|---|---|---|
| Polar | cool | cold | snow | near North and South Poles |
| Mountain | cool | cold | snow | on top of high mountains |
| Temperate | warm to hot | cool to cold | average | most land between tropical and polar regions |
| Tropical | hot | hot | heavy rain | most land around the equator |

1. Which climate zones are coldest? __polar and mountain__

2. Which climate zone is wettest? __tropical__

3. Which climate zone shows the most variation over a year? __temperate__

4. How did putting information in a chart help you compare the climate zones?
   __Possible answers include that it made it easier to see differences.__

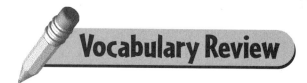

# Recognize Vocabulary

**Listed below are scrambled vocabulary terms. Use the clues to unscramble them. Write the unscrambled terms on the lines provided.**

**1.** D S L O W N L C I A
(2 words)

_____  horizontal movement of air resulting from local changes in temperature

**2.** N N O L E I
(2 words)

_____  short-term change in climate occurring around the Pacific Ocean every two to ten years

**3.** S T R P O E M H A E

_____  blanket of air surrounding Earth

**4.** O I R L C E I M M A T C

_____  the climate of a very small area

**5.** A E M T C L I

_____  the average of all weather conditions through all seasons over a period of time

**6.** P C E I I O N P T A T R I

_____  rain or snow

**7.** I I P N S V A G L N W I R E D
(2 words)

_____  global winds that blow constantly from the same direction and cover a large part of Earth's surface

**8.** B G L W A L M O G I R N A
(2 words)

_____  an abnormally rapid rise in Earth's average temperature caused by excess carbon dioxide in the atmosphere

**9.** A S R R E R I S U P E
(2 words)

_____  the weight of air

**10.** Y H M I I U T D

_____  water or moisture in the air

## Chapter 4 • Graphic Organizer for Chapter Concepts

Jetties

Name _____

Date _____

# Waves

## Materials

rectangular pan          water          straw

## Activity Procedure

1. **Make a model** of the ocean by half-filling the pan with water.

2. Place your straw near one side of the pan, and gently blow across the surface of the water. What happens?

3. **Observe** the height and speed of the waves you make. **Record** your observations.

4. Repeat Step 2 several times, blowing a little harder each time. What do you **observe** about the waves you make? **Record** your observations.

Name _____

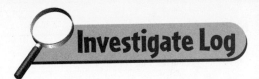

## Draw Conclusions

**1.** Use your observations to describe a relationship between how hard you blow and the height and speed of the waves. The harder you blow, the faster the waves move and the bigger they are.

_____

**2.** From what you observed in this activity, what can you **infer** about the cause of waves on oceans and other bodies of water? Waves are caused by wind.

_____

_____

**3. Scientists at Work** Scientists often **use models** to learn about things they connot **observe** directly. What did your model help you observe about waves? Waves are caused by wind; more wind causes faster and larger waves; waves move in the direction the wind is blowing.

_____

**Investigate Further  Predict** how high the waves on a pond, a lake, or the ocean will be on a calm day and on a stormy day. Then test your predictions by **using a model.** _____

_____

_____

_____

Name _____

Date _____

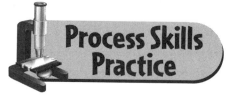

# Observe

You observe when you use your senses to note the properties of an object or event. You can observe directly, or you can use instruments such as microscopes or hand lenses.

## Think About Observing

When you observe something, you often ask questions about what you are observing. Observing then leads to other process skills, such as measuring, comparing, recording data, inferring, or drawing conclusions. Beneath the drawing below, you will see that some conclusions have been drawn. What can you observe in the drawing that would help you reach those conclusions?

| Conclusion | Observation |
|---|---|
| **1.** It is either morning or evening. | |
| **2.** It is dark under the water. | |
| **3.** The diver does not have to come to the surface to breathe and can probably stay underwater for a long while. | |

**Use with page C93.**

Name _____

Date _____

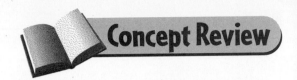 **Concept Review**

# How Do Ocean Waters Move?

## Lesson Concept

Ocean waters move as waves, currents, and tides. Most waves are caused by wind. Currents are caused by prevailing winds and differences in water temperature. Tides are caused by the gravitational pull of the sun and the moon.

## Vocabulary

| **wave** (C94) | **current** (C96) | **tide** (C98) |

**Choose the short answer that best completes each sentence below.**

**1.** Most of the movement of water on the ocean's surface is caused by _____ . *A*

   **A** waves       **B** currents       **C** tides

**2.** Earthquakes and volcanoes cause _____ . *A*

   **A** some of the       **B** some of the       **C** tropical
       biggest waves          strongest currents      storms

**3.** A stream of water that flows through the ocean like a river is called a _____ . *C*

   **A** rogue wave       **B** tsunami       **C** current

**4.** The Gulf Stream is a surface current that _____ . *B*

   **A** strikes the shore at      **B** carries warm water      **C** is a cold, deep-ocean
       an angle           to cold regions        current

**5.** Surface currents are caused by _____ . *C*

   **A** differences in water     **B** long ridges of sand     **C** prevailing winds
       temperature           that form near the
                  shoreline

**6.** Deep-ocean currents are caused by _____ . *A*

   **A** differences in water     **B** long ridges of sand     **C** prevailing winds
       temperature           that form near the
                  shoreline

**7.** Tides are caused by _____ . *B*

   **A** powerful deep-ocean     **B** the pull of gravity     **C** prevailing winds
       currents            from the sun and
               the moon

**Use with page C99.**

# The Effect of Waves on a Beach

## Materials

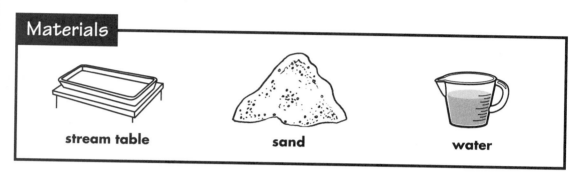

stream table          sand          water

## Activity Procedure

**1** Use sand to **make a model** of a beach at one end of the stream table. The beach should have a gentle slope.

**2** Slowly add water to the stream table until it is about half full. Try not to disturb the beach.

**3** Make a wave by lifting the sand end of the stream table about 2 cm above the tabletop and then dropping it. What do you **observe** about the beach and the water? Repeat this several times. **Record** your observations.

**4** Repeat Steps 1–3, but this time build a beach that is much steeper than the first one. **Record** your observations.

Name _____

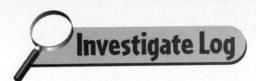 

## Draw Conclusions

**1.** Use your observations to explain how waves affect a beach. The beach erodes and the water becomes tan or brown in color as it mixes with the eroded sand.

**2.** Does the slope of the beach matter? Explain. Yes, the beach with the gentle slope will not erode as fast as the beach with the steep slope.

_____

**3. Scientists at Work** Scientists often **make a model** to study how natural processes work. How did your model help you **observe** how waves affect a beach? The model demonstrates how waves might move sand or dirt to and from the beach.

_____

What couldn't you observe about wave action with your model?
The model couldn't show wave action over a long period of time.

_____

_____

**Investigate Further** If possible, study the shore of a pond, a lake, or an ocean in your area. What do you **observe** about the shore? What questions do you have about how waves affect the shore? **Plan and conduct a simple investigation** to help you answer your questions. Decide what equipment you will need to use in your investigation. _____

_____

_____

Name _____

Date _____

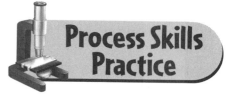

# Use a Model

Sometimes the best way to investigate a process is to make and use a model. This is especially true when you want to take a closer look at large-scale Earth processes such as ocean currents.

## Think About Using a Model

You have already learned that Earth's rotation causes ocean currents to bend to the right in the Northern Hemisphere and to the left in the Southern Hemisphere. You can model this effect with a very simple experiment. Suppose you are riding on a carousel and you have a tennis ball in your hand. You toss the ball to a friend who is standing in the grass beside the carousel.

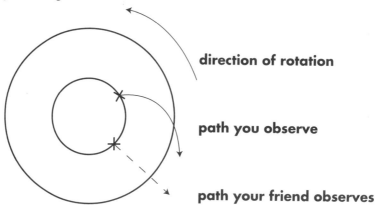

direction of rotation

path you observe

path your friend observes

× = **Your position on the carousel**

**1.** Does the path of the ball seem curved to your friend? _____

**2.** Why does the path seem curved to you? _____

_____

_____

**3.** Has some force acted on the ball to make its path curve? Explain.

_____

_____

**4.** How is this model like Earth and the ocean currents? How is it different?

_____

_____

_____

Name _____

Date _____

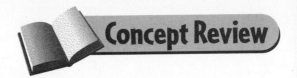

# How Do Oceans Interact with the Land?

## Lesson Concept

The shore is changed by waves, currents, and human activities. Waves erode beaches and cliffs, longshore currents deposit material along the shore, and human-made structures affect the natural process of shore change.

## Vocabulary

**shore** (C102)          **estuary** (C102)          **headland** (C103)

**tide pool** (C103)      **jetty** (C104)

Ocean waves, ocean currents, and human activity all have an effect on the shore. Read this list of things that can be done to the shore. Decide whether each one is the result of waves, currents, or human activity. Mark the effects of waves with a *W*. Mark the effects of currents with a *C*. Mark the effects of human activity with an *H*.

_____C,W_____ **1.** beach material being pushed along the shore

_____H_____ **2.** structures built to block longshore currents

_____W_____ **3.** rock along the shore slowly dissolved by a weak acid

_____C_____ **4.** the formation of sand spits by beach material that has been pulled sideways

_____H_____ **5.** jetties building up the beach by catching sand

_____W_____ **6.** the bottom of a cliff eroding, causing the cliff to break apart and fall into the ocean

_____H_____ **7.** structures built to protect beaches from erosion

_____W_____ **8.** pebbles and small rocks loosened through water pressure and carried out to the ocean

_____C,W_____ **9.** the formation of a new beach or the addition of material to an existing beach

# How Scientists Measure Ocean Depths

## Materials

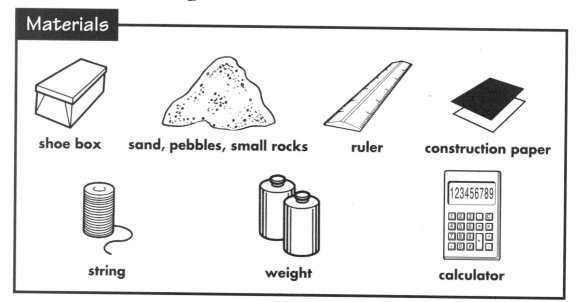

shoe box          sand, pebbles, small rocks          ruler          construction paper

string          weight          calculator

## Activity Procedure

**1** **Make a model** of the ocean floor by pouring sand and pebbles into the shoe box. Then scatter a few small rocks on top of the sand.

**2** Cut a piece of construction paper large enough to cover the top of the box. This will stand for the sea surface.

**3** With a pencil and ruler, draw a grid on the paper 4 squares wide by 8 squares long. Number the squares 1 through 32, and tape the lid onto the box. Tie the weight to a piece of string about twice as long as the box is deep.

**4** Make a hole in the first square in any row and lower the weighted end of the string until the weight just touches the ocean floor.

**5** Hold the string at sea level. **Measure** the length of string you pinched off to find the depth of the ocean. **Record** your measurement. Repeat Steps 4 and 5 for the remaining squares in that row.

**6** Use the Sonar Data table on page WB169. The "Time" is the number of seconds it takes for a sound to travel from a boat to the bottom of the ocean and back to the boat.

Name _____

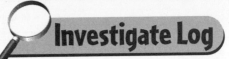 

WB169

**7** Use a calculator to multiply the Location 1 time by 1500 m/s (the speed of sound in water). Then divide the product by 2. This number is the depth of the water in meters at Location 1. This one has been done for you.

**8** Repeat Step 7 for each location in the table. Then make a line graph of the depths. The graph will be a profile of the ocean floor.

| Sonar Data | | |
|---|---|---|
| Location | Time (s) | Depth (m) |
| 1 | 1.8 | 1350 |
| 2 | 2.0 | 1500 |
| 3 | 3.6 | 2700 |
| 4 | 4.5 | 3375 |
| 5 | 5.3 | 3975 |
| 6 | 2.3 | 1725 |
| 7 | 3.1 | 2325 |
| 8 | 4.6 | 3450 |
| 9 | 5.0 | 3750 |
| 10 | 5.2 | 3900 |

## Draw Conclusions

1. Why do you think scientists today use sonar rather than weighted ropes to **measure** the depth of the ocean? Sonar is more accurate; sonar takes less time; weighted ropes aren't always long enough to reach the bottom.

_____

2. When using sonar, why must you divide each product by 2 to calculate the depth of the water? Sound waves must travel from the boat to the bottom of the ocean and then the same distance back again.

_____

3. **Scientists at Work** How could a scientist use sonar to **measure** the size of large objects on the ocean floor? by comparing data from several spots, looking for places where the depth is less

**Investigate Further** How could you find the depth of a pond, lake, or river? **Plan and conduct a simple investigation** to find out. Select the equipment you would need to use. _____

_____

_____

Process Skills
Practice

# Measure

When you measure something, you are determining what its length, weight, volume, or some other quality is. You do this by using measuring standards, such as meters, inches, grams, or pounds.

## Think About Measuring

Olden is a world where there are no roads, cars, airplanes, or any type of modern transportation. The only way to get from one place to another on Olden is by walking. The people who live there have no idea how big their world is. They have no idea what a mile or a kilometer is. They measure distance by the amount of time it takes to walk from one place to another.

**1.** Assuming that it takes you about one hour to walk two miles, how would you tell someone living on Olden that you live one mile away from school?

_____

**2.** How would you describe the distance between New York and Chicago, which is about 800 miles? _____

_____

**3.** Finish the table by filling in the Olden units of distance (that is, time) between New York and the cities listed in the left column.

|                          | **Miles** | **Olden Units** |
|--------------------------|-----------|-----------------|
| Cincinnati to New York   | 600       |                 |
| Indianapolis to New York | 700       |                 |
| Little Rock to New York  | 1300      |                 |
| Las Vegas to New York    | 2500      |                 |

**4.** Scientists on Earth use a unit called a light-year to measure the distances between the stars. Light travels about 186,000 miles in one second. What do you think a light-year is? _____

_____

_____

Use with page C107.

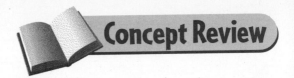
# How Do People Explore the Oceans and Use Ocean Resources?

## Lesson Concept

A wide range of technology is used to explore the ocean, including scuba equipment, submersibles, satellites, and sonar. The oceans contain valuable natural resources, such as fish, petroleum, minerals, and sea water.

## Vocabulary

**scuba** (C109)   **sonar** (C109)   **submersible** (C109)   **desalination** (C112)

Match the dates in the left column with the events in the right column. Write the letter of the event that matches each date in the space next to the date.

___D___ 1690

___F___ 1872

___B___ 1912

___I___ 1942

___G___ 1956

___A___ 1960

___C___ 1977

___H___ 1986

___E___ 1987

**A** Jacques Piccard and Donald Walsh go down to the deepest place in the Pacific Ocean (10, 920 m) in the *Trieste II*.

**B** The RMS *Titanic* strikes an iceberg in the North Atlantic and sinks to the bottom of the ocean.

**C** Scientists in *Alvin* discover hot springs deep under the ocean. The springs come from vents in the ocean floor over volcanically active areas.

**D** Sir Edmund Halley, an English astronomer, builds a diving bell that traps air for divers to use.

**E** *Nautile* brings up some objects from the *Titanic* wreck.

**F** Six scientists spend more than three years at sea on the voyage of the HMS *Challenger*.

**G** Allyn Vine convinces the United States government that scientists need deep-diving vessels that can hold small crews.

**H** *Alvin* is used to explore the wreckage of the sunken RMS *Titanic*.

**I** French explorer Jacques Cousteau invents an aqua-lung that allows a diver to move about freely under water to a depth of about 100 m.

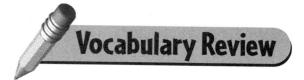

# Recognize Vocabulary

Look at the vocabulary terms in the box. Choose the term that best completes each sentence. Write your answers on the lines. Use each term only once.

| | | | |
|---|---|---|---|
| wave | scuba | headland | jetty |
| desalination | shore | tide pool | sonar |
| current | tide | submersible | |

I love to go to the beach. It's fun to splash in a (up-and-down movement of surface water) _____, but there's a lot more to do at the (area where the ocean and land meet and interact) _____.

I look for stuff washed up from distant lands by a (stream of water that flows through the ocean) _____. Once I found a can with writing I couldn't read! The (rise and fall in ocean level) _____ makes the beach look different at different times of day. I study the variety of plants and animals in a (pool of sea water found along a rocky shoreline) _____. Some days we climb the (process of hard rock left behind after softer rock has eroded) _____, exploring caves and other formations, and we walk out along the (wall of rocks that sticks out into the ocean) _____ to enjoy the crash of the sea and wind.

The ocean is an important resource. In some places people use (process of removing salt from sea water) _____ to provide water for drinking.

Next year, I'm going to take lessons on how to dive using (self-contained underwater breathing apparatus) _____ gear. When I get older, I want to be an oceanographer. I hope some day I'll be able to use (reflected sound waves) _____ to learn more about the ocean depths. Maybe I'll get to travel in a (small underwater vehicle) _____ to learn more about the mysteries of the deep!

Name _____  Date _____

## Chapter 1 • Graphic Organizer for Chapter Concepts

## Earth, Moon, and Beyond

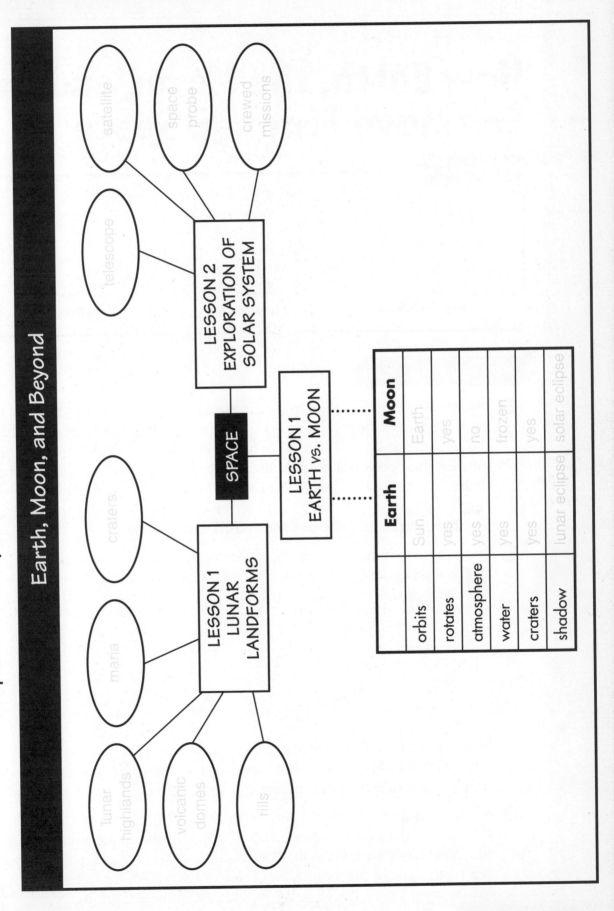

| | Earth | Moon |
|---|---|---|
| orbits | Sun | Earth |
| rotates | yes | yes |
| atmosphere | yes | no |
| water | yes | frozen |
| craters | yes | yes |
| shadow | lunar eclipse | solar eclipse |

# How Earth, the Moon, and the Sun Move Through Space

## Materials

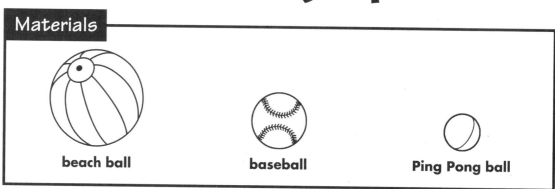

beach ball          baseball          Ping Pong ball

## Activity Procedure

**1** You will work in a group of four to **make a model** of the sun, Earth, and the moon in space. One person should stand in the center of a large open area and hold the beach ball over his or her head. The beach ball stands for the sun. A second person should stand far from the "sun" and hold the baseball overhead. The baseball stands for Earth. The third person should hold the Ping Pong ball near "Earth." The Ping Pong ball stands for the moon. The fourth person should **observe** and **record** what happens.

**2** The real Earth moves around the sun in a path like a circle that has been pulled a little at both ends. This shape, called an *ellipse* (ee•LIPS), is shown below.

For the model, Earth should move around the sun in an ellipse-shaped path. Earth should also spin slowly as it moves around the sun. The observer should **record** this motion.

**3** While Earth spins and moves around the sun, the moon should move around Earth in another ellipse-shaped path. The moon should also spin once as it moves around Earth. The same side of the moon should always face Earth. That is, the moon should spin once for each complete path it takes around Earth. The observer should **record** these motions.

Name _____

## Draw Conclusions

**1.** Your model shows three periods of time—a year, a month, and a day. Think about the time it takes Earth to spin once, the moon to move around Earth once, and Earth to move around the sun once. Which period of time does each movement stand for? Earth moving once around the sun—a year; the moon moving once around Earth—a month; Earth spinning around once—a day.

**2. Compare** the movements of the moon to the movements of Earth.
Possible answers: The moon and Earth spin at different speeds; the moon orbits the Earth, while Earth orbits the sun; the same side of the moon is always facing Earth.

**3. Scientists at Work** Scientists often **make models** to show **time and space relationships** in the natural world. However, models can't always show these relationships exactly. How was your model of Earth, the moon, and the sun limited in what it showed? Possible answer: Earth did not spin exactly 365 times as it moved around the sun once.

**Investigate Further** You could **make a model** to show how the sun shines on Earth. **Plan and conduct a simple investigation** to show how the amount of sunlight reaching Earth changes as Earth moves around the sun.

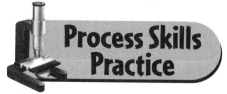

# Use Time and Space Relationships

Time relationships tell you the order of events. Space relationships tell you about locations of objects. Understanding these relationships can help you make accurate models.

## Think About Using Time and Space Relationships

Suppose you are a space traveler from Earth and you have just discovered a new solar system. You want to make an accurate map for those who will follow you. Answer these questions to plan your map. Use a separate sheet of paper if you need more space.

**1.** Think about mapping a new solar system. What space relationships will you show? _____

_____

_____

**2.** Seven large objects orbit a single star. Three of them have smaller objects orbiting them. What do the locations of the orbits tell you about the objects?

_____

_____

**3.** One of the seven larger orbiting objects is very close to the star. Three are a little farther away. Three are very far away. In which group are you most likely to find a planet to colonize? Explain. _____

_____

**4.** Why is it important to show the locations of the planets accurately?

_____

_____

_____

**5.** What would happen if you made a mistake in showing the locations of some of the planets or moons? _____

_____

_____

**Use with page D5.**

Name _____

Date _____

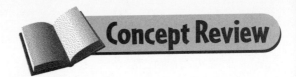

# How Do Earth and the Moon Compare?

## Lesson Concept

The moon revolves around Earth. The Earth-moon system revolves around the sun. Both Earth and the moon rotate on axes and have day-night cycles. Many features on Earth and the moon are different, but some landforms occur on both.

## Vocabulary

**revolve** (D6)         **orbit** (D7)         **rotate** (D7)

**axis** (D7)            **eclipse** (D8)

Select words from the box below to label the diagram. Watch out! Not every word in the box can be used to label the diagram, so you'll have to pick and choose.

| | | | | |
|---|---|---|---|---|
| lunar mare | gibbous | orbit | moon | full moon |
| day-night cycle | sun | Earth | eclipse | crater |
| quarter moon | half moon | axes | revolve | rotation |

Name _____

Date _____

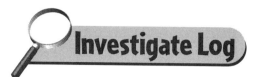 

# The Moon's Craters

## Materials

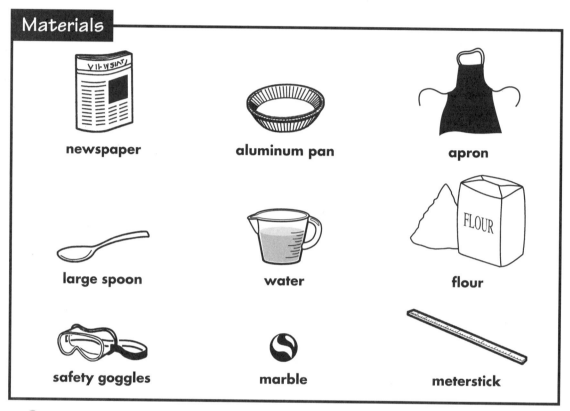

newspaper

aluminum pan

apron

large spoon

water

flour

safety goggles

marble

meterstick

 CAUTION

## Activity Procedure

**1** Use the following table.

| Trial | Height | Width of Craters |
|-------|--------|------------------|
| 1 | 20 cm | |
| 2 | 40 cm | |
| 3 | 80 cm | |
| 4 | 100 cm | |

**2** Put the newspaper on the floor. Place the pan in the center of the newspaper.

**3** Use a large spoon to mix the water and flour in the aluminum pan. The look and feel of the mixture should be like thick cake batter. Now lightly cover the surface of the mixture with dry flour.

**4** **CAUTION** **Put on the safety goggles and apron** to protect your eyes and clothes from flour dust. Drop the marble into the pan from a height of 20 cm.

**Investigate Log**

5 Carefully remove the marble and **measure** the width of the crater. **Record** the measurement in the table. Repeat Steps 4 and 5 two more times.

6 Now drop the marble three times each from heights of 40 cm, 80 cm, and 100 cm. Measure the craters and record the measurements after each drop.

## Draw Conclusions

1. **Compare** the height from which each marble was dropped to the size of the crater it made. How does height affect crater size? The greater the height, the wider the crater.

2. The Copernicus (koh•PER•nih•kuhs) crater on the moon is 91 km across. Based on your model, what can you **infer** about the object that formed this crater? The object came from a great distance or it was very large.

3. **Scientists at Work** Most of the moon's craters were formed millions of years ago. Scientists **use models** to **infer** events that occurred too long ago to **observe** directly. What did you infer from the model about how the moon's craters formed? The moon's craters formed when its surface was hit by objects from space.

**Investigate Further Hypothesize** how using larger or smaller marbles would affect the size and shape of the craters. **Plan and conduct a simple investigation** to test your hypothesis. _____

_____

_____

_____

_____

Process Skills
Practice

# Infer

You infer when you use logical reasoning to draw conclusions based on observations. An inference based on logical reasoning and observation is always valid, even though it may not be correct.

## Think About Inferring

Imagine you are in a spacecraft flying over the surface of an unexplored planet that is about the same size as Earth. Crewless probes have reported that the planet is composed of material that is common to both the moon and Earth. You are the first human to see this planet. Looking down through thin, moving clouds, you notice that there are craters and a lot of areas that look like the maria of the moon. Most of the craters look worn and old, but a few have high, sharp sides and look new. Some of the craters have steam rising from them and are surrounded by a plain made of fresh material. Others are in rougher areas and are surrounded by material that has been thrown out over the ground. You also notice very large fields of what look like sand dunes.

1. From your observations of the new planet, what can you infer about how the craters were formed? Explain. _____

_____

_____

_____

_____

2. What can you infer about life on this planet? _____

_____

_____

_____

_____

3. What can you infer about weather on this planet? _____

_____

_____

_____

_____

**Use with page D13.**

Name _____

Date _____

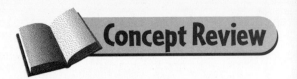

# How Have People Explored the Solar System?

## Lesson Concept

People have studied objects in space since ancient times. They began by using their unaided eye and then the telescope. Today they also use satellites and space probes. In the future, people may live and work on space stations and moon bases.

## Vocabulary

**telescope** (D15)          **satellite** (D15)          **space probe** (D16)

**Write the letter of an event next to the year it occurred.**

_D_ 900

_F_ 1609

_H_ 1668

_I_ 1936

_A_ 1957

_C_ 1961

_G_ 1969

_B_ 1977

_E_ 1981

**A** The Soviet Union launches *Sputnik 1*, the first artificial satellite.

**B** *Voyager I* and *Voyager II* space probes are launched. They have sent back pictures of Jupiter, Saturn, Uranus, and Neptune and are traveling beyond the solar system.

**C** The Mercury program sends the first Americans into space.

**D** Mayan people build an observatory for viewing the stars and planets at Chichén Itzá, in Mexico, around this date.

**E** Beginning of the use of space shuttles to lift heavy cargoes into orbit; to provide labs for scientific research in space; and to launch, bring back, and repair satellites

**F** Galileo uses a telescope to observe four moons orbiting Jupiter.

**G** American astronaut Neil Armstrong is the first person to walk on the moon.

**H** Sir Isaac Newton designs a telescope that uses a mirror as well as lenses to produce sharper images than those produced by Galileo's telescope.

**I** The first radio telescope is built and detects radio waves coming from objects in space.

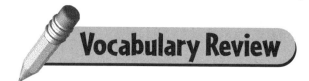
# Recognize Vocabulary

Read the following sentences. On each line, write the letter for the word or phrase that could be substituted for the vocabulary term in italics.

_____ 1. In 1609 Galileo used a *telescope* to observe craters on the moon.
  **A** artificial satellite
  **B** robot vehicle used to explore space
  **C** instrument that makes distant objects appear nearer

_____ 2. As it travels around the sun, Earth *rotates*.
  **A** spins on its axis
  **B** travels in a closed path
  **C** moves in an ellipse

_____ 3. The *Voyager space probes* have sent pictures of distant planets back to Earth.
  **A** artificial satellites
  **B** robot vehicles used to explore space
  **C** instruments that make distant objects appear nearer

_____ 4. Earth's *axis* travels through its North Pole and South Pole.
  **A** imaginary line that passes through Earth's center
  **B** elliptical path that Earth travels around the sun
  **C** shadow that Earth casts over the moon at some points in its orbit

_____ 5. Gravity makes the Earth-moon system *revolve* around the sun.
  **A** spin on its axis
  **B** travel in a closed path
  **C** face the sun as it moves

_____ 6. A total lunar *eclipse* lasts more than two hours and can be seen from any place on Earth that is facing the moon.
  **A** passage through Earth's shadow
  **B** trip around Earth in an elliptical path
  **C** volcanic eruption that leaves pools of dark lava on the moon

_____ 7. Earth's *orbit* around the sun is an ellipse, a shape that is nearly but not quite circular.
  **A** path as it revolves
  **B** imaginary line that passes through the center and the poles
  **C** shadow cast that causes an eclipse

# Chapter 2 • Graphic Organizer for Chapter Concepts

## The Sun and Other Stars

Name _____

Date _____

# Sunspots

## Materials

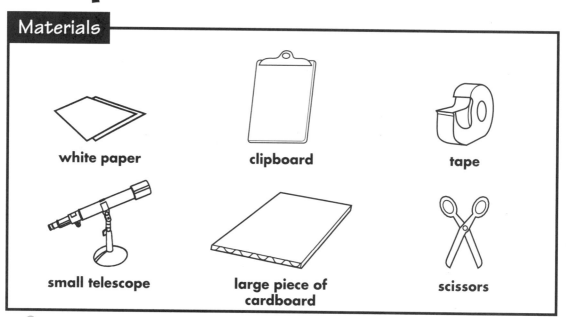

white paper

clipboard

tape

small telescope

large piece of
cardboard

scissors

## CAUTION Activity Procedure

1. **CAUTION** **Never look directly at the sun. You can cause permanent damage to your eyes.** Fasten the white paper to the clipboard. Tape the edges down to keep the wind from blowing them.

2. Center the eyepiece of the telescope on the cardboard, and trace around the eyepiece.

3. Cut out the circle, and fit the eyepiece into the hole. The cardboard will help block some of the light and make a shadow on the paper.

4. Point the telescope at the sun, and focus the sun's image on the white paper. **Observe** the image of the sun on the paper.

5. On the paper, outline the image of the sun. Shade in any dark spots you see. The dark spots are called *sunspots*. **Record** the date and time on the paper. **Predict** what will happen to the sunspots in the next day or two. *Note:* Since the image of the sun on the paper is reversed, any movement you **observe** will also be reversed. For example, movement from east to west, or from right to left on the image, represents movement from west to east on the sun.

6. Repeat Step 5 each sunny day for several days. **Record** the date, the time, and the positions of the sunspots each day.

Name _____

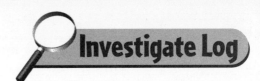 

## Draw Conclusions

**1.** How did the positions of the sunspots change over several days?

The sunspots should have moved across the paper from right to left until

reaching the left side of the image.

_____

_____

_____

**2.** What can you **infer** from the movement of sunspots? Since sunspots move

across the sun's surface from west to east, right to left on the paper, students

can conclude that the sun rotates from west to east.

_____

_____

_____

_____

**3. Scientists at Work** Scientists **draw conclusions** from what they **observe**. Galileo
was the first scientist to observe that it takes a sunspot about two weeks to cross
from the left side of the sun's surface to the right side. Two weeks later, the
sunspot appears on the left side of the sun's surface again. From this information,
what conclusions can you draw about the time it takes the sun to make one

complete rotation? about four weeks

_____

_____

**Investigate Further** Does the sun always have the same number of spots?
Do sunspots change in size? **Plan and conduct a simple investigation** to find
answers to these and any other questions you might have about sunspots.

_____

_____

_____

_____

_____

_____

_____

Name _____

Date _____

# Draw Conclusions

Drawing conclusions involves the use of other process skills, such as observing. Unlike inferences, conclusions are usually based on much more data and should be tested repeatedly.

## Think About Drawing Conclusions

In ancient times two astronomers were watching sunspots. The first astronomer concluded the spots were planets orbiting the sun. The second astronomer watched the sunspots more closely than the first. He noticed the spots changed shape as they approached the edge of the sun's image. They became compressed and then seemed to disappear. The second astronomer concluded the spots were part of the sun's surface.

**1.** Why do you think the two astronomers came to such different conclusions?

_____

_____

**2.** What other data could the astronomers have gathered to support their

conclusions? _____

_____

_____

**3.** Astronomers over the ages have kept records of sunspots. The following is a graph showing the appearance of sunspots from 1900 to 2000. What

conclusions can you draw from the graph? _____

_____

_____

Name _____

Date _____

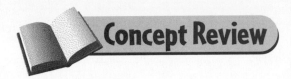

# What Are the Features of the Sun?

## Lesson Concept

The sun is the source of almost all the energy on Earth. The sun has layers and visible surface features.

## Vocabulary

| | | |
|---|---|---|
| **photosphere** (D33) | **corona** (D33) | **sunspot** (D34) |
| **solar flare** (D34) | **solar wind** (D34) | |

Vocabulary terms and other words from this lesson are listed in the chart below. Choose the correct term for each blank attached to a part of this diagram of the sun.

| | | | |
|---|---|---|---|
| **corona** | **core** | **solar flare** | **convection zone** |
| **solar wind** | **photosphere** | **sunspot** | **radiation zone** |

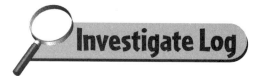

# The Brightness of Stars

## Materials

lamp with 40-watt bulb          lamp with 60-watt bulb

## Activity Procedure

**1** Place the two lamps near the middle of a darkened hall. Turn the lamps on.

**2** **Observe** the lamps from one end of the hall. **Compare** how bright they look. **Record** your observations.

**3** Move the lamp with the 60-watt bulb to one end of the hall. **Observe** and **compare** how bright the two lamps look from the other end of the hall. **Record** your observations.

**4** Now place the lamps side by side at one end of the hall. Again **observe** and **compare** how bright the two lamps look from the other end of the hall. **Record** your observations.

**5** **Predict** the distances at which the two lamps will seem to be equally bright. **Experiment** by placing the lamps at various places in the hall. **Observe** and **compare** how bright the two lamps look from a variety of distances. **Record** your observations.

Name _____

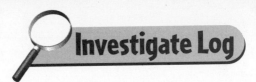
Investigate Log

## Draw Conclusions

**1.** What two variables did you test in this experiment? how bright the light
actually is and how far it is from the observer

_____

_____

**2.** From what you **observed**, what two factors affect how bright a light appears to
an observer? distance and brightness

_____

_____

**3.** **Scientists at Work**  Scientists often **draw conclusions** when **experimenting**.
Use the results of your experiment to draw conclusions about how distance
and actual brightness affect how bright stars appear to observers on Earth.
Possible answer: If two stars have the same brightness, the star that is
farther away appears less bright than the nearer star. If a dimmer star is
closer, it can look as bright as a brighter star that is farther away.

_____

_____

_____

**Investigate Further**  Why can't you see stars during the day? Use the lamps and a
brightly lighted room. **Plan and conduct a simple investigation** to show how the
sun can make it seem that stars don't shine during the day. _____

_____

_____

_____

_____

# Experiment and Draw Conclusions

You draw conclusions after you have experimented and collected data.
Drawing conclusions is usually the last step in an investigative process.
When you draw a conclusion, you pull together what you have learned
from observation or experimentation.

## Think About Experimenting and Drawing Conclusions

You are involved in a search for extraterrestrial
intelligence. You build a gigantic radio antenna
on top of the highest building near your home.
You let it scan the sky, hoping someone on another
planet is sending signals to Earth. After you
experiment with your antenna, you begin
gathering data and drawing conclusions.

1. You receive a burst of radio noise, called static, at the same time every day. You
   suspect it's coming from a local radio station. Can you draw any conclusions?

   Explain. _____

   _____

2. You notice the radio noise is coming from a fixed point in the sky and is
   actually a series of pulses. If you keep your antenna aimed at that spot, the
   pulses continue without stopping. Can you draw any conclusions? Explain.

   _____

   _____

3. You aim a telescope at the source of the pulses and see a small white star. Can
   you draw any conclusions? Explain. _____

   _____

   _____

4. You check a star map. The star you have been observing is a pulsar, which is a
   star that spins very, very fast and sends out a radio signal as it spins. Can you

   draw any conclusions? Explain. _____

   _____

Name _____

Date _____

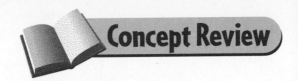
Concept Review

# How Are Stars Classified?

Stars are classified by absolute magnitude, surface temperature, size, and color. Stars change from nebula to protostar to main-sequence star to expanding star to red giant to planetary nebula and white dwarf. Most stars are main-sequence stars.

## Vocabulary

**magnitude** (D38)                    **main sequence** (D39)

Match the star type in Column A with its description in Column B by writing the letter of the correct description next to the star type.

### Column A

___C___ main-sequence star

___F___ nebula

___G___ red giant

___A___ expanding star

___B___ planetary nebula

___E___ protostar

___D___ white dwarf

### Column B

**A** An object with the mass of the sun shines for billions of years. Then, as its hydrogen runs low, it starts to get bigger.

**B** The star's atmosphere expands a million times.

**C** After several million years, the temperature at the center of the object gets hot enough to release various kinds of energy.

**D** The object continues to shine dimly for billions of years as it slowly cools.

**E** Attracted to each other by gravity, the particles squeeze together. The object grows, gets hotter, and starts to glow.

**F** A star begins within a huge cloud of hydrogen, helium, and tiny particles of dust.

**G** The star may expand to 100 times its former size.

# The Sun's Location in the Milky Way Galaxy

## Materials

scrap paper

## Activity Procedure

1. Make about 70 small balls from scrap paper. These will be your "stars."

2. On a table, **make a model** of the Milky Way Galaxy. Arrange the paper stars in a spiral with six arms. Pile extra stars in the center of the spiral. Use fewer stars along the arms.

3. Look down at the model. Draw what you **observe**.

4. Position your eyes at table level. Look across the surface of the table at the model. Again, draw what you **observe**.

5. Look at the photographs at the bottom of page D47. One is of a spiral galaxy viewed from the edge. The other shows the galaxy viewed from the "top." **Compare** the pictures you drew in Steps 3 and 4 with the photographs of a spiral galaxy. Then look at page D46. **Observe** the photograph of a ribbon of stars. This is our view of the Milky Way Galaxy from Earth. Using your drawings and the photographs, **infer** where in the Milky Way Galaxy the sun is.

Name _____

## Draw Conclusions

**1.** Suppose the sun were located "above" the Milky Way Galaxy. What view of the galaxy might we see from Earth? We would see the arms of the spiral Milky Way Galaxy. _____

_____

_____

**2.** If the sun is in one of the arms, what view might we see of the galaxy then? We would see the Milky Way Galaxy as a ribbon of stars. _____

_____

_____

**3.** From your drawings and the photographs of a spiral galaxy, where in the Milky Way Galaxy do you **infer** the sun is? The sun is in one of the arms of the spiral Milky Way Galaxy. The side view students drew looks like the view from Earth.

_____

_____

_____

**4. Scientists at Work** Scientists often **infer** when **using models** like the one you made. How did your model of the Milky Way Galaxy help you infer the sun's location in the galaxy? A model helps you draw the Milky Way Galaxy from several points of view.

_____

_____

**Investigate Further Observe** the Milky Way Galaxy in the night sky. You will need a clear, dark night, far away from city lights. Binoculars or a telescope will help you see some of the fainter stars. _____

_____

_____

_____

_____

Name _____

Date _____

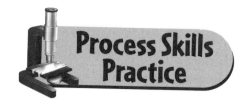

# Use Models

You can use a model to study something that is too big to study in your classroom. For example, you may use a wall chart to study the solar system, or projections of stars on the ceiling to study the night sky.

## Think About Using Models

When you want to see where you live in relation to the rest of the city, you can look at a map. A map is a model of your city. You can find the street you live on and, if the map is detailed enough, you can even figure out where your house is on the street. Astronomers have carefully measured the light from stars in our galaxy and have figured out how far away they are from the sun. They have used this information to draw maps of the galaxy as it would look from the side and from above.

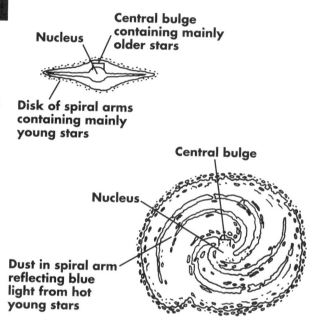

Central bulge containing mainly older stars

Nucleus

Disk of spiral arms containing mainly young stars

Central bulge

Nucleus

Dust in spiral arm reflecting blue light from hot young stars

1. Looking at the map, where in our galaxy do you think you would find most of the matter (that is, stars, gas, and dust)? _____

   _____

2. Which of the two views shown do you think most resembles the Milky Way Galaxy as seen from Earth? Explain. _____

   _____

   _____

3. The entire galaxy is rotating. The inner stars are moving faster than the outer stars. How fast is the sun moving when compared to the rest of the galaxy?

   _____

   _____

   _____

Use with page D45.

Name _____

Date _____

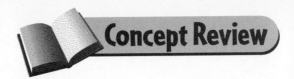

# What Are Galaxies?

## Lesson Concept

A galaxy is a group of stars, gas, and dust. The sun is in the Milky Way Galaxy, which is part of a galactic cluster called the Local Group.

## Vocabulary

**universe** (D46)     **galaxy** (D46)     **light-year** (D47)

**Answer each question with one or more complete sentences.**

**1.** How are galaxies classified? _Galaxies are classified by shape._

**2.** You are looking through your telescope at the night sky, and you see a pinwheel-shaped object. What do you think it is? _It's probably a spiral galaxy._

**3.** What shape do irregular galaxies have? _Irregular galaxies have no obvious shape._

**Mark the following statements with *True* or *False*. If the statement is false, write a correction next to it.**

__True__ **4.** Many galaxies rotate around a core. _____

__True__ **5.** A nebula has no light of its own. _____

__False__ **6.** A light-year is a unit of time. _A light-year is a unit of distance._

__False__ **7.** Most galaxies are elliptical. _About half of all galaxies are elliptical._

__False__ **8.** The Milky Way is an irregular galaxy. _The Milky Way is a spiral galaxy._

__True__ **9.** Elliptical galaxies probably don't rotate. _____

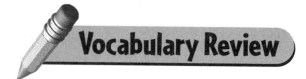
# Recognize Vocabulary

Listed below are the vocabulary terms from this chapter. Match the terms in Column A with the definitions in Column B by writing in the space next to the term the letter of the correct definition.

**Column A**

_____ 1. photosphere

_____ 2. corona

_____ 3. sunspot

_____ 4. solar flare

_____ 5. solar wind

_____ 6. magnitude

_____ 7. main sequence

_____ 8. universe

_____ 9. galaxy

_____ 10. light-year

**Column B**

**A** a fast-moving stream of particles released into space from the surface of the sun

**B** dark places on the surface of the sun that are cooler than the areas surrounding them

**C** the brightness of a star

**D** the part of the sun that we see

**E** everything that exists: planets, stars, dust, gases, and energy

**F** a group of stars, gas, and dust

**G** the sun's atmosphere

**H** the distance light travels in one Earth year, about 9.5 trillion kilometers

**I** the most common combinations of color, size, magnitude, and temperature of stars; plotted on a special diagram, they appear in a band stretching from the upper left of the diagram to the lower right

**J** brief burst of energy from the sun's atmosphere

# Chapter 1 • Graphic Organizer for Chapter Concepts

## Matter and Its Properties

### LESSON 1
### PHYSICAL PROPERTIES

1. mass _____
2. weight _____
3. volume _____
4. density _____
5. solubility _____

### LESSON 2
### CHANGES OF STATE

1. melting _____
2. freezing _____
3. boiling _____
4. condensation _____
5. sublimation _____
6. evaporation _____

### LESSON 3
### CHEMICAL PROPERTIES

1. reactivity _____
2. combustibility _____

# Using Physical Properties to Identify Objects

## Materials

apples     ruler     balance     string

## Activity Procedure

**1** Carefully **observe** the apple your teacher gave you. What properties of your apple can you discover just by observing it? **Record** all the properties you observe.

**2** Use the balance, ruler, and string to **measure** some characteristics of your apple. **Record** the properties you measure.

**3** Put your apple in the pile of apples on your teacher's desk. Don't watch while your teacher mixes up the apples.

**4** Using the properties that you recorded, try to identify your apple in the pile.

**5** Using the balance, ruler, and string, **measure** this apple. **Compare** the measurements to those you recorded earlier. Then decide whether the apple you chose from the pile is yours. If someone else chose the same apple, comparing measurements should help you decide whose apple it really is.

Name _____

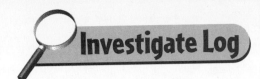
Investigate Log

## Draw Conclusions

1. **Compare** your apple with a classmate's apple. How are the two apples alike? How are they different? _Answers will vary._

   _____

   _____

2. Why was it helpful to **measure** some characteristics of your apple in addition to **observing** it? _Measuring characteristics gives definite values._
   _Observations can vary, even for the same object._

   _____

3. How did you use the string to **measure** the apple? _wrapped the string_
   _around the apple and then measured the string to find the circumference of_
   _the apple_

4. **Scientists at Work** Scientists use both observations and measurements to identify substances. Which is faster, **observing** or **measuring**? Which provides more exact information? _Observing is usually faster, but measuring_
   _provides more definite characteristics._

   _____

**Investigate Further** **Compare** the list of your apple's properties with a classmate's list. Then, using your classmate's list, try to find his or her apple. Talk with your classmate about how he or she made the list. Did you and your classmate do things the same way? _____

   _____

   _____

   _____

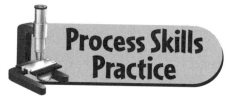

# Observe and Measure

Observing is learning facts about something by using your senses.
Measuring, a form of observation, is learning facts by using
instruments that can be used to extend your senses.

## Think About Observing and Measuring

Tanya's science teacher told the class that chemical elements do not break down
during normal laboratory reactions. Then she said that the iron in fortified cereal
is not an iron compound, but pure iron! To demonstrate, she poured the contents
of a box of iron-fortified cereal into a large bowl and crushed the cereal into a
powder. She mixed water into the powder until it was very thin
and watery. Then she took a small bar magnet taped to a
glass rod and stirred the cereal and water mixture
for several minutes. When she pulled the bar
magnet out, tiny bits of iron were clinging to it.

1. Tanya observed the iron clinging to the magnet. How could her class measure

   the amount of iron in the box of cereal? _____

   _____

   _____

2. Tanya and her classmates read on the side panel of the cereal box that one
   serving of the cereal met the recommended daily allowance for iron and that
   one cup of cereal was one serving. What observation and measurement could
   they do to see if the cereal really provided the recommended daily allowance

   for iron? _____

   _____

   _____

   _____

   _____

3. How did the iron become separated from the cereal? Did the chemical elements
   of the cereal break down when Tanya's teacher mixed it with water? Explain.

   _____

   _____

   _____

Name _____

Date _____

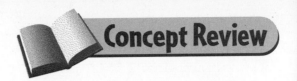

# How Can Physical Properties Be Used to Identify Matter?

## Lesson Concept

Matter has mass and takes up space. Physical properties can be used to identify different types of substances. Some physical properties, such as mass, volume, and density, can be measured.

## Vocabulary

| | | | |
|---|---|---|---|
| **matter** (E6) | **physical properties** (E6) | **mass** (E7) | **weight** (E7) |
| **volume** (E8) | **density** (E9) | **solubility** (E10) | |

**Choose the answer that best completes the statement.**

**1.** The effect of gravity on matter is the measure of ___B___.

  **A** mass        **B** weight        **C** density

**2.** An object has a mass of 120 g on Earth. On the moon it would have a mass of ___C___.

  **A** 20 g        **B** 60 g        **C** 120 g

**3.** The density of a steel hammer is 7.9 $g/cm^3$ on Earth. On a spaceship it would have a density of ___C___.

  **A** 0 $g/cm^3$        **B** 3.9 $g/cm^3$        **C** 7.9 $g/cm^3$.

**4.** Matter is anything that has mass and ___A___.

  **A** occupies space        **B** properties        **C** size

**Decide whether the underlined term makes each statement true or false. If the statement is true, write the word *true* on the line. If the statement is false, write a word or phrase that makes the statement true.**

_____are not_____ **5.** Materials <u>are</u> changed when physical properties are measured.

_____true_____ **6.** A milliliter is a unit of <u>volume</u>.

_____solution_____ **7.** In a <u>mixture</u>, the particles are evenly mixed.

# Changing States of Matter

## Materials

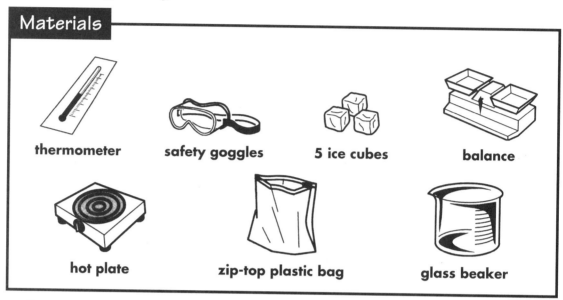

thermometer    safety goggles    5 ice cubes    balance

hot plate    zip-top plastic bag    glass beaker

CAUTION

## Activity Procedure

1. Place five ice cubes in a zip-top plastic bag. Be sure to seal the bag. Use the balance to **measure** the mass of the ice cubes and the bag. **Observe** the shape of the ice cubes. **Record** your observations and measurements.

2. Set the bag of ice cubes in a warm place. **Observe** what happens to the shape of the ice cubes. Use the balance to **measure** the mass of the melted ice cubes and the bag. Unzip the bag slightly and insert the thermometer. Measure the temperature of the water. **Record** your observations and measurements. Use your observations to **infer** that a change of state is occurring.

3. After the ice has completely melted, pour the water into a glass beaker. Put the thermometer in the beaker. **Observe** what happens to the water's shape, and **record** the water's temperature.

4. **CAUTION** **Put on the safety goggles.** Your teacher will use a hot plate to heat the water in the beaker until it boils. **Observe** what happens to the water when it boils. **Record** the temperature of the boiling water. Use your observations to **infer** that another change of state has occurred.

Name _____

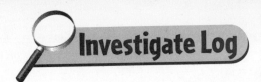 

## Draw Conclusions

1. Identify the different states of water at different points in this investigation.
The ice cubes and the melted ice water are obvious. The water vapor cannot
be seen. Be sure students understand that the steam from the boiling water
is not water vapor, but condensed water vapor.

_____

2. **Compare** the mass of the ice to the mass of water after it melted. What does
this show about changes in state? The mass is the same. Changes in state do
not cause changes in mass.

_____

3. What temperatures did you **record** as the water changed states?
Accept answers within reasonable temperature range.

_____

4. **Scientists at Work**  After scientists use their senses to **observe** the properties of
substances, they can **infer** whether a change in state has taken place. What did
you observe in this investigation? What did you infer about a change of state
from each observation? changes in the state and shape of water; that energy in
some form is present

_____

**Investigate Further**  The physical change that happens to water when it is boiled
produces water vapor—an invisible gas. **Plan and conduct a simple investigation**
to test the hypothesis that the mass of the water vapor is the same as the mass of
the liquid water. Accept reasonable answers.

_____

_____

_____

_____

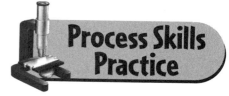

# Observe and Infer

Observation is collecting information about something by using your senses. Inferences are assumptions you make after considering your observations. Observations are facts, but inferences are guesses and may not always be correct.

## Think About Observing and Inferring

Every night Dan could hear strange creaking noises in his bedroom and from the hallway outside his door. He finally asked his father about the noises and if the house was haunted. "That's just the house," explained his father. When Dan seemed doubtful, his father reached into the recycle bin and found a long-necked bottle. "After the sun goes down," he explained to Dan, "the house cools and contracts, that is, it actually gets smaller." To demonstrate, he partially inflated a balloon and put it over the bottle's neck as shown in the drawing. When he put the bottle into a bowl of ice water, the balloon shrank and fell over. When he put the bottle outside in the sun, the balloon slowly became inflated again.

1. What was Dan's first inference when he observed the noises in his house? Was his observation a fact? Was his inference correct? _____

   _____

2. What did he observe about the balloon and the bottle? _____

   _____

   _____

3. Why would Dan's house make noise expanding and contracting although the balloon did not? _____

   _____

   _____

Name _____

Date _____

Concept Review

# How Does Matter Change from One State to Another?

## Lesson Concept

Three states of matter are solid, liquid, and gas. Changes in state are physical changes. Particles of matter move faster as heat is added and slow down as heat is removed. Every substance has a melting point, the temperature at which it changes from a solid to a liquid. It also has a boiling point, the temperature at which it changes from a liquid to a gas.

## Vocabulary

**solid** (E14)          **liquid** (E14)          **gas** (E14)

**evaporation** (E16)     **condensation** (E17)

Identify the following characteristics as belonging to solids (S), liquids (L), or gases (G). Some characteristics belong to more than one state of matter.

__S__ **1.** particles are held rigidly in place

__L, G__ **2.** takes the shape of the container

__S__ **3.** has a definite shape

__S, L__ **4.** particles are touching

__L__ **5.** particles slide over one another

__G__ **6.** particles are far apart

Choose the answer that best completes the statement.

**7.** The freezing point of a substance is the same as its __A__ point.
   **A** melting       **B** boiling       **C** condensation

**8.** Evaporation changes a __C__.
   **A** gas to a liquid     **B** liquid to a solid     **C** liquid to a gas

**9.** When a substance freezes, it __B__.
   **A** gains energy     **B** loses energy     **C** stays the same

**10.** Boiling involves the same change of state as __C__.
   **A** freezing     **B** condensation     **C** evaporation

Name _____

Date _____

Investigate Log

# Chemical Properties

## Materials

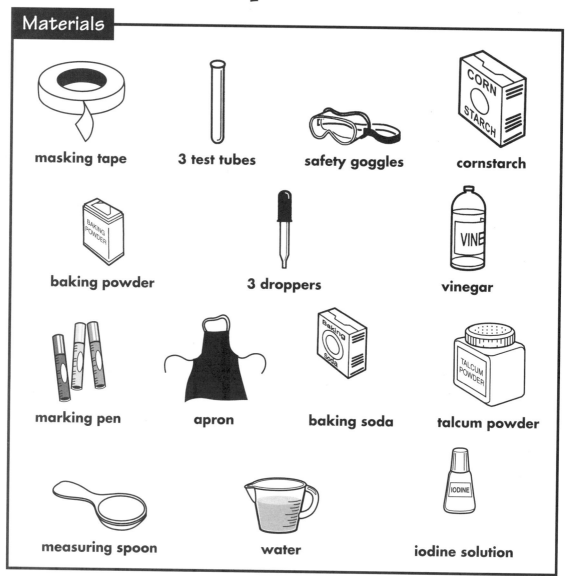

masking tape     3 test tubes     safety goggles     cornstarch

baking powder     3 droppers     vinegar

marking pen     apron     baking soda     talcum powder

measuring spoon     water     iodine solution

CAUTION    **Activity Procedure**

**1** Use the masking tape and marking pen to label your test tubes *water*, *vinegar*, and *iodine*.

**2** **CAUTION** Put on the apron and safety goggles. Leave them on for the entire activity.

**3** Put about $\frac{1}{3}$ spoonful of baking soda in each test tube. Add a dropper of water to the test tube labeled *water*. **Observe** and **record** what happens.

**4** Add a dropper of vinegar to the test tube labeled *vinegar*. **Observe** and **record** what happens this time.

**5** Add a dropper of iodine solution to the test tube labeled *iodine*. **CAUTION** Iodine is poisonous if swallowed and can cause stains. Be careful not to spill or touch the iodine solution. Wash your hands if you get iodine on them. **Observe** and **record** what happens.

**6** Wash the test tubes with soap and water. Repeat Steps 3–5 three more times using cornstarch, talcum powder, and baking powder in the test tubes instead of baking soda. Be sure to wash the test tubes between tests. **Observe** and **record** what happens each time.

**7** Get an "unknown" sample from your teacher. It will be one of the substances you have already tested. Test it with water, vinegar, and iodine solution, just as you did before. **Observe** and **record** what happens when you add each of the liquids. What is your unknown substance?

## Draw Conclusions

1. How did you find out what your unknown sample was? _by comparing the way it reacted with the way the known samples react_

2. Vinegar is one of a group of substances called *acids*. Acids react with substances called *bases*. Of the substances you tested, which are bases? How can you tell? _baking soda and baking powder, because they reacted with the vinegar_

3. Baking powder is not a pure substance. It is a mixture of two of the other substances you tested. Based on your results, what do you **infer** are the two substances in baking powder? _baking soda and cornstarch_

4. **Scientists at Work** Scientists **experiment** to find out if two substances react. What signs of reactions did your experiments produce? What **variables** did you **control**? _A change in color and bubbling were evidence of a reaction; the quantity of substances and drops used._

**Investigate Further** Suppose you wanted to discover some of the chemical properties of chalk. **Predict** whether chalk is an acid or a base. Then **experiment** to test your prediction. _____

_____

_____

_____

_____

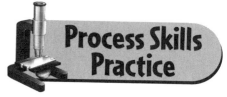

# Experiment

One of the most basic of all activities in science is experimenting. Scientists state hypotheses and then design experiments to test them. Scientists change certain conditions in experiments and observe what happens. From these observations, they can see whether their hypotheses were correct.

## Think About Experimenting

Sandra learned in science class that each substance has its own characteristic properties. One of those properties is density. Her teacher also said that the properties of a substance do not change even if the sample size changes. Sandra found that hard to believe. Sandra knew she could measure the density of a substance by putting it in water. If something floats, it is less dense than water. If it sinks, it is more dense than water. Sandra put some water in a clear jar and dropped in a piece of potato. The potato floated. Sandra hypothesized that a large enough piece of potato would sink. She put a large potato in the water and it also floated.

**1.** What was Sandra's hypothesis? _____

_____

_____

**2.** What did Sandra observe? Was her hypothesis supported by her experiment?

Why or why not? _____

_____

_____

_____

**3.** If the potato floats, then it is less dense than the water. Hypothesize what would happen if you could somehow make the potato more dense.

_____

_____

**4.** Design an experiment that would test your hypothesis. _____

_____

_____

_____

_____

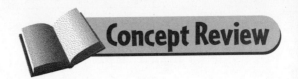

Concept Review

# How Does Matter React Chemically?

## Lesson Concept

Physical changes do not result in the formation of new substances. However, new substances are formed during chemical changes. Physical and chemical properties can be used to identify substances and to separate mixtures. Matter is neither produced nor destroyed during physical and chemical reactions.

## Vocabulary

**reactivity** (E23)                    **combustibility** (E24)

**Answer each question with one or more complete sentences.**

**1.** What is the difference between a physical change and a chemical change?
In a physical change, the original substance remains. In a chemical change, new substances are formed.

**2.** If you had a mixture of two substances and had your choice of using a physical change or a chemical change to separate them, which would you prefer? Explain. Probably a physical change because both substances could be recovered. In a chemical change, at least one substance would be changed into something else.

**3.** What is the relationship between the chemical properties of a substance and the chemical changes of a substance? The chemical properties of a substance, such as reactivity, determine what chemical changes it will undergo.

**Identify each of the following as a physical or chemical change by writing** *physical* **or** *chemical* **on the line.**

**4.** a snow bank shrinking on a cold day          physical

**5.** forming a bar of gold into wire          physical

**6.** bleaching a sheet and pillowcase          chemical

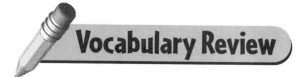
# Recognize Vocabulary

**Match the term on the left with its description on the right by
writing the letter of the description in the blank next to the term.**

_____ **1.** matter

_____ **2.** solid

_____ **3.** liquid

_____ **4.** physical
properties

_____ **5.** gas

_____ **6.** mass

_____ **7.** evaporation

_____ **8.** weight

_____ **9.** condensation

_____ **10.** volume

_____ **11.** reactivity

_____ **12.** density

_____ **13.** combustibility

_____ **14.** solubility

**A** the state of matter that has no definite shape
or volume

**B** the pull of gravity on matter

**C** changing from a gas to a liquid

**D** the amount of matter in an object

**E** the ability of a substance to dissolve

**F** the changing of a liquid to a gas

**G** the ability of a substance to react chemically

**H** the characteristics of a substance that can be
measured without changing the substance

**I** mass per unit of volume

**J** the state of matter with a definite shape
and volume

**K** the ability to burn

**L** anything that has mass and occupies space

**M** the amount of space anything occupies

**N** the state of matter with a definite volume but
no definite shape

Name _____ Date _____

## Chapter 2 • Graphic Organizer for Chapter Concepts

## Atoms and Elements

# Mystery Boxes

## Materials

| sealed box provided by your teacher | ruler | balance | magnet |

## Activity Procedure

**1** With a partner, **observe** the sealed box your teacher gave you. **Record** any observations you think might help you learn about what's inside the box.

**My observations:** _____

**2** Use the ruler to **measure** the outside of the box. Use the balance to find the mass of the box. **Record** your results.

**My measurements:** _____

**3** Carefully tilt and shake the box. How many objects do you **infer** are in the box? How big do you infer the objects are? **Record** your inferences and the reasons for them.

**My inferences:** _____

**4** Hold the magnet to the surface of the box. Then tilt the box. Are any of the objects in the box attracted to the magnet? Repeat this at several places on the surface of the box.

**My observations:** _____

**5** What objects do you **infer** are inside the box? Base your inferences on your measurements and observations.

**My inferences:** _____

**6** What do you **infer** about the inside of the box? Draw a picture of what you think the inside of the box looks like.

**7** Now open the box. **Compare** your inferences about the objects in the box with the objects the box really contains. Also compare your inferences about what the box looks like inside with what it really looks like.

My comparisons: _____

_____

_____

## Draw Conclusions

**1.** How did what you **inferred** about the objects inside the box **compare** with what was really inside? Students should point out both correct and incorrect inferences.

**2.** How did what you **inferred** about the inside of the box **compare** with the way it really looked inside? Students should point out both correct and incorrect inferences.

**3.** **Scientists at Work** Different scientists may **infer** different things about objects they can't **observe** directly. Compare your inferences about the contents and the inside of the box with the inferences of other pairs. How were your inferences similar? How were they different? Groups probably made many different inferences about the contents and structure of the box.

**Investigate Further** Construct your own mystery box, and place various objects inside it. Give your box to a classmate. Your classmate will **observe** the box and **infer** things about its contents and how it looks inside.

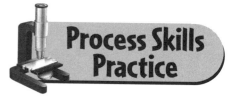

Process Skills Practice

# Observe and Infer

When you observe, you use one or more of your senses to perceive properties of objects and events. Observations can be made directly with the senses or indirectly through the use of instruments. When you infer, you use logical reasoning to draw conclusions based on observations. Inferences are explanations based on judgments and are not always correct.

## Think About Observing and Inferring

During the investigation activity, you observed and inferred the characteristics of a mystery box. Below are some of the things you did during the investigation. After each action, write an *O* if you were observing or an *I* if you were inferring when you performed that step.

| | |
|---|---|
| **1.** recorded things you noticed about the box | |
| **2.** used a ruler to measure the outside of the box | |
| **3.** listened to the sounds made and noticed the shifts in weight within the box when you tilted it and shook it | |
| **4.** drew a picture of what you thought the inside of the box looked like before you opened the box | |

**5.** How did observing help you make an inference about the box?

_____

_____

_____

**6.** Suppose you receive a large envelope in the mail. Before opening it, you observe it and infer what is in it. What might you observe about the envelope?

_____

_____

_____

**7.** What are some things you could infer about an unopened letter?

_____

_____

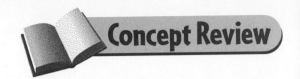
# What Are Atoms and Elements?

## Lesson Concept

Atoms are tiny particles of matter. Elements are substances made up of only one kind of atom.

## Vocabulary

| | | | |
|---|---|---|---|
| **nucleus** (E39) | **proton** (E39) | **neutron** (E39) | **electron** (E39) |
| **element** (E40) | **atom** (E40) | **molecule** (E40) | |

Below is a list of terms and names from this lesson. Put each term or name into the correct category by writing it under one of the headings below.

| | | | |
|---|---|---|---|
| **heat conductor** | **ductile** | **sodium** | **electron** |
| **iron** | **oxygen** | **Dalton** | **neutron** |
| **silicon** | **proton** | **malleable** | **Bohr** |
| **electrical conductor** | | | |

| Subatomic Particles | Common Elements | Properties of Metals | Scientists Who Studied Atoms |
|---|---|---|---|
| neutron | iron | ductile | Bohr |
| proton | silicon | malleable | Dalton |
| electron | oxygen | electrical conductor | |
| | sodium | heat conductor | |

Draw a picture of Bohr's model of an atom, and label each part.

# Grouping Elements

## Materials

aluminum foil          copper wire      steel (iron) paper clip      lead solder

sulfur          graphite pencil "lead"      helium-filled balloon

CAUTION  ## Activity Procedure

**1** Use the chart below to **record** the properties of the elements you **observe**.

| Object | Element | Phase | Color | Luster | Malleability |
|---|---|---|---|---|---|
| foil | | | | | |
| wire | | | | | |
| paper clip | | | | | |
| sulfur | | | | | |
| graphite | | | | | |
| solder | | | | | |
| balloon | | | | | |

**2** What elements do the objects represent? **Record** your answers in the second column of the chart.

**3** **Observe** each element. Is it a solid, a liquid, or a gas at room temperature? **Record** your observations in the column labeled "Phase" of the chart.

**4** What is the color of each element?
(Carefully release some of the helium from the balloon.) **Record** what you **observe** in the chart.

**5** Which elements have luster? (Which are shiny?) **Record** what you **observe** in the fifth column of the chart.

**6** Which elements bend easily? **Record** what you **observe** in the column labeled "Malleability." CAUTION **Wash your hands after handling the objects in this investigation.**

## Draw Conclusions

**1.** What similar properties did you **observe** in different elements?
Answers may include that aluminum, iron, and lead are silver-colored and
shiny; that aluminum, copper, iron, and lead are bendable; and that sulfur and
carbon are dull and don't bend.

**2.** Consider the properties you **observed** to form groups. Which elements could
you group together? Explain. _____ Aluminum, copper, iron, and lead; sulfur and
carbon; reasons might include luster and bendability.

**3. Scientists at Work** Scientists have made a periodic table, in which elements are grouped by their properties. Using your observations, **predict** which elements from the activity are near each other in the periodic table. _____ Students should
suggest that the elements they grouped together should be near each other
in the periodic table.

**Investigate Further** Think of other properties that could be used to group elements. Are there any you could test? **Plan and conduct a simple investigation** of one group of elements from this activity using these new tests.
Additional properties that students may test include magnetism, electrical and
thermal conductivity, and melting point.

Process Skills
Practice

# Observe and Predict

You can use observations to predict the outcomes of future events.
Before making scientific predictions, you should think about previous
observations you made of related events.

## Think About Observing and Predicting

Observe the table below. Each element in the table is shown with its
atomic number and atomic mass. The atomic mass is the mass of one
mole ($6.02 \times 10^{23}$ atoms) of an element.

| Element | Atomic Number | Atomic Mass in Grams |
|---------|:-------------:|:--------------------:|
| Helium | 2 | 4 |
| Carbon | 6 | 12 |
| Nitrogen | 7 | 14 |
| Oxygen | 8 | 16 |
| Sodium | 11 | |
| Iron | | 56 |

**1.** How many electrons circle around the nucleus of each atom of oxygen? _____

**2.** Describe the relationship between atomic number and atomic mass in

the table. _____

**3.** The atomic mass of sodium is missing. What would you predict the atomic

mass to be? _____

**4.** The atomic number of iron is missing. What would you predict the atomic

number to be? _____

**5.** The atomic mass of sodium is actually 23 g. The atomic number of iron is
actually 26. Compare these values to your predictions in Questions 3 and 4.
What does this tell you about the relationship you saw between atomic

number and atomic mass? _____

_____

_____

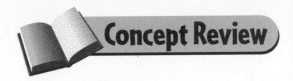
Concept Review

# What Are Compounds?

## Lesson Concept

Compounds are molecules made of two or more elements.

## Vocabulary

| periodic table (E47) | compound (E48) |

Chemists use shorthand to describe compounds. Use the table below to match each chemical symbol with the element it stands for.

| C = carbon | Ca = calcium | Cl = chlorine | H = hydrogen |
|---|---|---|---|
| He = helium | O = oxygen | N = nitrogen | Na = sodium |
| Fe = iron | | | |

1. One molecule of table salt (NaCl) has ___1___ atom(s) of
   _____sodium_____ and ___1___ atom(s) of _____chlorine_____.

2. One molecule of water ($H_2O$) has ___2___ atom(s) of _____hydrogen_____
   and ___1___ atom(s) of _____oxygen_____.

3. One molecule of methane ($CH_4$) has ___1___ atom(s) of
   _____carbon_____ and ___4___ atom(s) of _____hydrogen_____.

4. One molecule of ammonia ($NH_3$) has ___1___ atom(s) of
   _____nitrogen_____ and ___3___ atom(s) of _____hydrogen_____.

Circle the choice that best completes each sentence below.

5. The order of elements in the periodic table is based on the
   (number of protons in one atom) / atomic mass.

6. Elements with properties of metals and nonmetals are called
   (metalloids) / semi-metals.

7. A Russian chemist named Dmitri Mendeleev organized elements by
   atomic number / (atomic mass.)

Name _____

Date _____

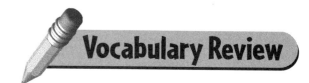

**Vocabulary Review**

# Recognize Vocabulary

**On the line, write the letter of the answer that best completes each sentence.**

1. The _____ is the center of an atom.
   **A** nucleus     **B** proton     **C** compound     **D** molecule

2. A(n) _____ is made up of only one kind of atom.
   **A** compound     **B** element     **C** molecule     **D** atomic number

3. A(n) _____ is a subatomic particle with a negative charge.
   **A** electron     **B** nucleus     **C** neutron     **D** proton

4. The smallest unit of an element that has all the properties of that element is a(n) _____.
   **A** substance     **B** compound     **C** atom     **D** molecule

5. The elements are arranged in order of atomic number in the _____ table.
   **A** atomic     **B** Mendeleev     **C** periodic     **D** atomic mass

6. A(n) _____ is made of atoms of two or more elements.
   **A** neutron     **B** compound     **C** element     **D** molecule

7. A(n) _____ is a subatomic particle with a positive charge.
   **A** electron     **B** nucleus     **C** neutron     **D** proton

8. When two or more atoms are linked together, they form a(n) _____.
   **A** substance     **B** compound     **C** atom     **D** molecule

9. A(n) _____ is a subatomic particle with no charge.
   **A** electron     **B** nucleus     **C** neutron     **D** proton

Name _____  Date _____

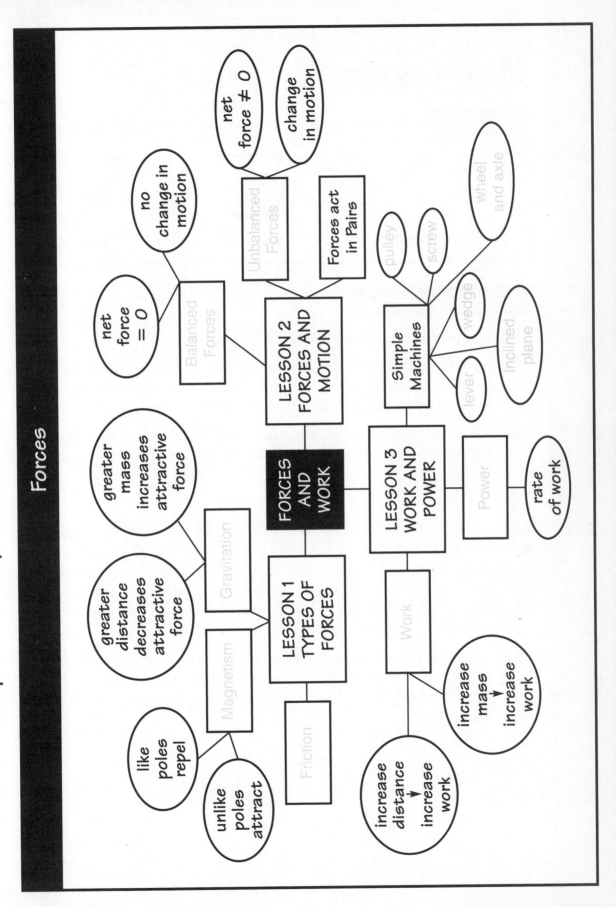

Forces

net force ≠ 0
change in motion
no change in motion
net force = 0
Unbalanced Forces
Forces act in Pairs
Balanced Forces
LESSON 2 FORCES AND MOTION
Simple Machines
pulley
screw
wheel and axle
wedge
inclined plane
lever
FORCES AND WORK
LESSON 3 WORK AND POWER
Power
rate of work
greater mass increases attractive force
greater distance decreases attractive force
Gravitation
LESSON 1 TYPES OF FORCES
Magnetism
Friction
Work
increase mass → increase work
increase distance → increase work
like poles repel
unlike poles attract

Name _____

Date _____

# Magnetism

## Materials

2 bar magnets      compass      test objects

## Activity Procedure

1. Use the chart on the next page for this activity.

2. From the group of objects, choose one to test. Write the name of the object on your chart. **Predict** whether this object will be attracted, or pulled, by one of the magnets. **Record** your prediction on your chart.

3. Place the object on a desk. Slide a magnet slowly toward the object until the magnet touches it. In your chart, **record** whether the object is attracted to the magnet or not.

4. Repeat Steps 2 and 3 for each of the test objects.

5. Bar magnets have two different ends, called poles. One is labeled *N* for north seeking, and the other is labeled *S* for south seeking. **Observe** what happens when you bring the north-seeking pole of one magnet near the south-seeking pole of another magnet. Then observe what happens when you bring two north-seeking poles or two south-seeking poles together. **Record** your observations.

6. Now place the compass on the desk. Slowly slide one of the magnets toward the compass. **Observe** what happens to the compass needle. Now move the magnet around the compass and observe what happens. **Record** your observations.

Name _____

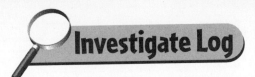 

| Object | Prediction | Test Result |
|--------|------------|-------------|
|        |            |             |
|        |            |             |
|        |            |             |
|        |            |             |

## Draw Conclusions

**1.** What characteristic of an object determines whether or not it is attracted by a magnet? Some metallic objects are attracted by magnets; or iron objects are attracted by magnets.

_____

**2.** **Infer** what characteristic of a compass needle accounts for your observations of the compass and the magnet. Students may infer that a compass needle is also a magnet.

_____

**3.** **Scientists at Work** Scientists often **hypothesize** about why things happen. Then they **plan and conduct investigations** to test their hypotheses. Form a hypothesis about why unlike magnetic poles attract each other while like magnetic poles repel, or push away, each other. Then plan and conduct an investigation to test your hypothesis. Students' hypotheses should relate to the magnetic fields around the magnets. Their investigations should use magnets and iron filings to show the shapes of these fields around like and unlike poles.

**Investigate Further** Research to find out why a compass needle always points to the north. Students may bring in compasses to prove the validity of this statement.

_____

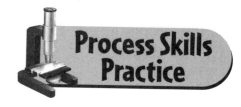

# Hypothesize

When you hypothesize, you make an educated guess about the relationship between variables. A hypothesis must be something that can be tested. A hypothesis is often changed because of the outcome of experiments that test it.

## Think About Hypothesizing

Leona's mother bought a small car because lightweight cars can go farther than heavy cars on the same amount of gasoline. Because weight is important to fuel efficiency, Leona wondered how the weight of the gasoline itself affects gas mileage. She hypothesized that a car probably gets better gas mileage when it has less gas in it. Therefore, to save both gas and money, it is better to fill the gas tank half-full than to fill it full. Her mother suggested they experiment to test the hypothesis.

1. How could Leona test her hypothesis? _____

_____

_____

_____

_____

_____

2. What are some variables in this experiment? _____

_____

_____

3. Which of the variables should be held constant in this experiment?

_____

4 What results would support Leona's hypothesis? _____

_____

5. Suppose Leona and her mother discovered that their gas mileage increased by 0.5 mile per gallon of gas by driving with the tank half-full. How much more often would they have to stop at the gas station to get this extra mileage? Do you think it would be worth the extra stops at the gas station?

_____

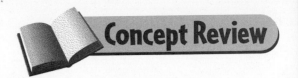
**Concept Review**

# What Forces Affect Objects on Earth Every Day?

## Lesson Concept

A force is a push or a pull that can move an object, stop it, or change its direction. Some forces are direct; others work at a distance. Where two surfaces rub against each other, the force of friction opposes motion. Magnetism pulls the poles of magnets together or pushes them apart. Gravity, which pulls objects toward each other, depends on the masses of the objects and how far apart they are.

## Vocabulary

**force** (F6)     **friction** (F6)     **magnetism** (F7)     **gravitation** (F8)

**Complete each sentence below by writing the word *friction*, *magnetism*, or *gravitation* in the blank.**

1. The moving parts of an automobile engine are coated in oil or grease to reduce the _____friction_____ between the metal parts.

2. Some toys let you draw hair, eyebrows, and other features with a special wand that moves iron filings around by _____magnetism_____.

3. A balance scale works by using _____gravitation_____ to compare the weights of two objects.

4. A parachute uses the force of air pushing up on a large area of silk to resist the force of _____gravitation_____.

5. When you apply the brakes on your bike, you are clamping down on the bike's wheel to increase the force of _____friction_____.

6. Hikers can use a compass to guide them along a trail because the compass needle is pulled to the north by _____magnetism_____.

7. You can tape lightweight objects to a wall, but if you try to tape something heavy to a wall and it falls off, you'll know the tape isn't strong enough to overcome the force of _____gravitation_____.

# Forces That Interact

## Materials

clipboard       tape       spring       marker

graph paper       ring stand       weight

## Activity Procedure

**1** Tape the graph paper to the clipboard. Across the bottom of the graph paper, draw a line and label it *Seconds*. Starting at one end of the line, make a mark every 2.5 cm.

**2** Attach the spring to the ring stand. Then attach the weight to the free end of the spring. Tape the marker to the bottom of the weight so that its tip points toward the back of the setup.

**3** Have a partner hold the clipboard with the graph paper taped to it behind the weight. The marker point should just touch the graph paper. Pull the weight until the spring is fully stretched.

**4** Have your partner slide the clipboard across a table at a steady rate of about 2.5 cm per second. As soon as the clipboard starts to move, drop the weight. As it bounces, it traces its movements on the graph paper.

**5** **Interpret the data** on your graph. Identify and mark the points where the weight was not moving up or down for an instant. Identify and mark the direction (up or down) the weight was moving along each sloping line. Identify and mark the places where the weight was moving most rapidly.

Name _____

## Draw Conclusions

**1.** At what points was the weight not moving? _at the top and bottom of each_
_cycle_

_____

**2.** At what point was the weight moving most rapidly? _at the midpoint of each_
_cycle_

_____

**3.** From your graph, **infer** the point at which the force of the spring was the
greatest. _at the bottom of each cycle_

_____

**4. Scientists at Work** Scientists often **draw conclusions** after they **interpret data**
they have collected. After studying your graph, draw conclusions to answer the
following questions:

During which part of each cycle was the force of gravity greater than the force
of the spring? _the downward half of each cycle_

_____

During which part of each cycle was the force of the spring greater than the
force of gravity? _the upward half of each cycle_

_____

**Investigate Further Hypothesize** how your graph would look if you repeated the
activity with a heavier weight. **Plan and conduct a simple investigation** to test
your hypothesis. _Encourage students to formulate testable hypotheses and_
_select and use appropriate equipment. Ask students to analyze and critique_
_the strengths and weaknesses of their hypotheses based on their results._

_____

_____

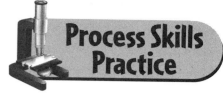

# Interpret Data and Draw Conclusions

When you interpret data, you look for patterns or meaning in information that is given to you or information you have gathered from your own observations.

## Think About Interpreting Data and Drawing Conclusions

The table below shows the force required to lift various objects on Earth as well as on two other planets, Planet X and Planet Y. The force is expressed in newtons (N). Study the data table, and then answer the questions that follow.

| Force Needed to Lift Objects | | | | |
|---|---|---|---|---|
| Object | On Earth (N) | On Planet X (N) | On Planet Y (N) | Mass (g) |
| 1 | 20.0 | 8 | 4 | 2040.8 |
| 2 | 7.5 | 3 | 1.5 | 765.3 |
| 3 | 12.5 | 5 | 2.5 | 1275.5 |
| 4 | 5.0 | 2 | 1 | 510.2 |
| 5 | 25.0 | 10 | 5 | 2551.0 |

1. Which of the three planets has the strongest gravitational pull? Explain.

   _____

2. Which of the three planets has the weakest gravitational pull? Explain.

   _____

3. List the objects in order, starting with the one having the greatest mass and ending with the one having the least mass. _____

4. How did you use your knowledge of interpreting data to help you decide what the information in the data table means? _____

   _____

   _____

   _____

Name _____

Date _____

# What Are Balanced and Unbalanced Forces?

## Lesson Concept

Balanced forces occur when two forces acting on an object are equal in size and opposite in direction. Unbalanced forces occur when forces acting on the same object are not opposite and equal. When forces are unbalanced, a net force occurs, causing acceleration. When you calculate the net force on an object, you must account for both the size and the direction of the forces.

## Vocabulary

| | |
|---|---|
| **balanced forces** (F12) | **unbalanced forces** (F13) |
| **acceleration** (F13) | **net force** (F14) |

**Decide whether the underlined term or phrase makes each statement true or false. If the statement is true, write the word *true* on the line. If the statement is false, write a word or phrase that makes the statement true.**

_true_ **1.** <u>Balanced</u> forces are equal in size and opposite in direction and therefore cancel each other out.

_true_ **2.** The change in motion of an object is always caused by <u>a force or forces</u>.

_no force_ **3.** If balanced forces are acting on an object, it will seem as if <u>a net force</u> is acting on the object.

_in pairs_ **4.** Forces always act <u>alone</u>.

_adding or subtracting_ **5.** <u>Balancing</u> the forces acting on an object gives you the net force.

_unbalanced_ **6.** When <u>balanced</u> forces act on an object, the object speeds up, starts to move, slows down, stops, or changes direction.

_true_ **7.** If <u>two equal forces</u> act on an object in opposite directions, the net force will be balanced.

_true_ **8.** <u>Unbalanced forces</u> can stop a moving object.

Name _____

Date _____

# Measuring Work

## Materials

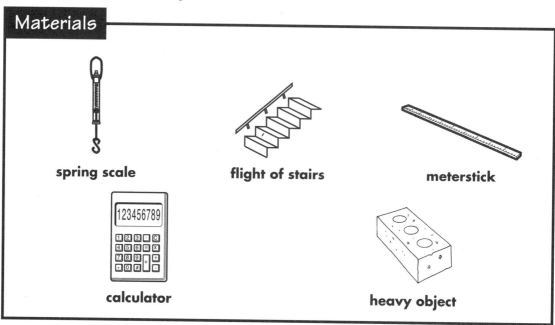

spring scale     flight of stairs     meterstick

calculator     heavy object

## Activity Procedure

**1** Use the table below for this activity.

**2** Weigh the object using the spring scale and **record** its weight in the table, next to *Trial 1*.

| | Work | | |
|---|---|---|---|
| **Trial** | **Weight (newtons)** | **Height (meters)** | **Work (joules)** |
| 1 | | | |
| 2 | | | |
| 3 | | | |
| 4 | | | |

**3** **Measure** the total height of the flight of stairs in meters. **Record** the measurement in your table, also next to *Trial 1*.

**4** Work can be **measured** as the product of force (in newtons) and distance (in meters). **Calculate** to find the number of newton-meters, or *joules*, of work you would do if you carried the object up the flight of stairs. **Record** the product in the table.

**5** Suppose you carried the object up two flights of stairs. Beside *Trial 2* on the table, **record** the new height and **calculate** the work done.

**6** For *Trial 3*, **calculate** how much work you would do if you carried the object up three flights every day for a week.

**7** For *Trial 4*, suppose your weight is 300 newtons. **Record** this new data and **calculate** the work you do climbing the stairs without carrying the object.

## Draw Conclusions

1. **Compare** the amount of work a person weighing 300 newtons does climbing one flight of stairs to the total amount of work the same person does climbing three flights of stairs every day for a week. Twenty-one times as much work is done in a week.

2. **Interpret** your **data** and **draw conclusions** about how work is related to force and distance. As force or distance increases, the amount of work done also increases.

3. **Scientists at Work** When scientists **interpret data**, they often **draw conclusions** based on the data they collected. What can you conclude about the amount of work done by people who weigh more than 300 newtons? they do more work

**Investigate Further** *Power* is the measure of how quickly work is done. You can measure power in *joules per second*. **Plan and conduct a simple investigation** to calculate how much power you use walking up a flight of stairs compared to running up a flight of stairs. _____

_____

_____

_____

# Interpret Data

When you interpret data, you look for patterns or meaning in information that has been given to you or information that you have gathered.

## Think About Interpreting Data

The table below provides data about five students who participated in a fitness test. Look at the data, and then answer the questions that follow.

| Name | Student Weight | Distance Run | Time |
|------|----------------|--------------|------|
| Darcy | 369 N | 500 m | 120 seconds |
| Carla | 392 N | 500 m | 116 seconds |
| Tyler | 400 N | 500 m | 122 seconds |
| Tasha | 382 N | 500 m | 126 seconds |
| Daniel | 419 N | 500 m | 130 seconds |

1. Which of the five students requires the most force to move his or her body? Explain. _____

_____

2. Which of the five students did the most work? Explain. _____

_____

_____

3. Write a mathematical sentence that describes the amount of work done by Daniel. _____

4. Which student is the most powerful? Explain. _____

_____

_____

5. How did having the data in a table help you interpret it to answer the questions?

_____

_____

_____

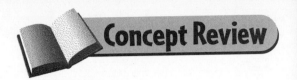
Concept Review

# What Is Work and How Is It Measured?

## Lesson Concept

Work is the force applied to an object times the distance the object is moved. Work is measured in joules. Power is a measure of the speed at which work is done. Power is measured in watts. Machines are devices that make work seem easier by changing the size or direction of a force. Pulleys, levers, wheels and axles, inclined planes, wedges, and screws are simple machines.

| Vocabulary | | |
| --- | --- | --- |
| **work** (F18) | **power** (F19) | **machine** (F20) |

Rewrite the descriptions in Questions 1–4 as mathematical sentences. Express values in newtons (N), meters (m), joules (J), and watts (W). Do any calculations necessary to find these values.

1. Vanessa and her father have built a sandbox for a neighborhood playground. They need to fill the sandbox with 20 bags of sand. Each bag weighs 50 pounds. How many newtons of force will be needed to lift the sand? _50 lb × 20 bags_

   _= 1000 lb ; 1000 lb × 4.5 = 4500 N_

2. The closest Vanessa and her father can get the back of their truck to the sandbox is 5 meters. How much work will Vanessa and her father have to do to move all the sand to the sandbox? _4500 N × 5 m = 22,500 J_

3. Figure out how much work Vanessa's father must do to move one bag of sand.

   _50 lb × 4.5 = 225 N × 5 m = 1125 J_

4. It takes Vanessa's father three minutes to lift one bag of sand from the truck and carry it to the sandbox. How much power does Vanessa's father use to move one bag of sand?

   _3 min × 60 sec/min = 180 sec; 1125 J ÷ 180 sec = 6.25 J per_

   _second = 6.25 W_

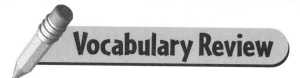
# Recognize Vocabulary

Choose from the following terms to solve each riddle. Use each term only once.

| | | | |
|---|---|---|---|
| balanced forces | work | power | forces |
| net force | magnetism | acceleration | gravitation |
| friction | machines | unbalanced forces | |

_____ **1.** I am a repulsing force, and my partner is an attracting force. Together we are forces between the poles of a magnet. What are we?

_____ **2.** I am a force pushing on an object, and you are a force pushing back on the object, but neither of us is moving the object. What are we?

_____ **3.** When you catch a football and run with it, I am what you are doing when you move the ball and yourself over the distance you run. What am I?

_____ **4.** We can change force into distance and distance into force. What are we?

_____ **5.** We are pushes or pulls. What are we?

_____ **6.** The faster you work, the more you have of me. What am I?

_____ **7.** I am a force, I oppose motion, and you find me where the surfaces of two objects meet. What am I?

_____ **8.** We are both pulling the same object in opposite directions. At first the object doesn't move. Then it does. What are we when the object moves?

_____ **9.** I am the force that keeps your feet on the ground. What am I?

_____ **10.** I am a way of measuring the effect of two forces on an object.

_____ **11.** I am a change in movement, caused by unbalanced forces. What am I?

Name _____  Date _____

# Chapter 2 • Graphic Organizer for Chapter Concepts

## Motion

### LESSON 1
### WAYS TO DESCRIBE MOTION

Speed

Velocity

Acceleration

1. _____

2. _____

3. _____

### LESSON 2
### THE THREE LAWS OF MOTION

First Law: An object at rest will

remain at rest, and an object in

motion will continue to move in a

straight line at a constant speed

until an outside force acts on it.

Second Law: An object's

acceleration depends on the size

and direction of the force acting on it

and the mass of the object.

Third Law: For every action force,

there is an equal and opposite

reaction force.

### LESSON 3
### WHY PLANETS STAY IN ORBIT

Law of Universal Gravitation:

All objects in the universe are

attracted to all other objects.

# Changes in Motion

## Materials

clear pastic bottle
with cap

water

small piece
of soap

## Activity Procedure

**1** Fill the bottle nearly to the top with water. Leave only enough space for a small air bubble. Add a small piece of soap to the water. This will keep the air bubble from sticking to the side of the bottle. Put the cap tightly on the bottle.

**2** Lay the bottle on its side on a flat surface. You should see one small bubble in the bottle. Hold the bottle steady until the bubble moves to the center of the bottle and stays there.

**3** **Predict** what will happen to the air bubble if you turn the bottle to the left or right. Turn the bottle and **observe** what happens. **Record** your observations.

**4** Now **predict** what will happen to the air bubble if you move the bottle straight ahead at a steady speed. Move the bottle and **observe** what happens. **Record** your observations.

**5** Repeat Step 4, but this time slowly increase the bottle's speed. **Observe** happens to the air bubble. **Record** your observations.

Name _____

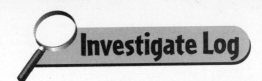
## Draw Conclusions

**1. Compare** your predictions and your observations. What happened when you
turned the bottle to the left or right, or moved it forward? The bubble moved
in the same direction as the bottle.

_____

**2.** From what you **observed**, how did a change in speed affect the bubble?
A change in speed caused the bubble to move in the direction of the change.

_____

**3. Scientists at Work** Were you surprised by the way the air bubble moved?
When scientists get surprising results, they often **hypothesize** about the cause
of those results. Form a hypothesis about why the bubble moves the way it
does. Students' hypotheses should include the idea that the bubble moves in
reaction to the water. As the bottle moves, the water tends to stay where it is
at first, pushing the bubble in the direction of the movement.

_____

**Investigate Further  Predict** what will happen to the air bubble if the bottle is
moving at a steady speed and its direction changes. **Plan and conduct a simple**

**investigation** to test your prediction. _____

_____

_____

_____

_____

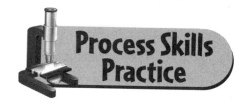

# Hypothesize

When you hypothesize, you make an educated guess about the relationships between variables. A hypothesis must be something you can test in an experiment, and it may be proven wrong in an experiment. A hypothesis is based upon observation, prior knowledge, and prior experimental outcomes.

## Think About Hypothesizing

Suppose you want to find out the effect of an inclined surface on an object's speed. In addition to a stopwatch, you have the following materials to work with:

a smooth board, 15 centimeters wide by 30 centimeters long

a cylindrical glass jar weighing 75 grams

a cylindrical glass jar weighing 150 grams

2 blocks of wood, 2 centimeters thick

2 blocks of wood, 4 centimeters thick

1. State a hypothesis about how the slope of an inclined surface might affect an object's speed. _____

_____

2. Describe an experiment, using the materials listed above, that would test this hypothesis. _____

_____

_____

3. State a hypothesis about how the weight of a jar might affect its speed down the inclined board. _____

_____

4. Describe an experiment that would test your hypothesis. _____

_____

_____

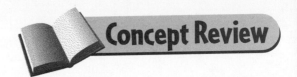

# How Are Motion and Speed Related?

## Lesson Concept

Motion is a change in an object's position. Speed is a measure of the distance an object moves in a given amount of time. Velocity is speed in a particular direction. Acceleration is a change in velocity, either in direction or in speed. Momentum, the product of an object's velocity and its mass, is a measure of how hard it is to slow down or stop an object.

## Vocabulary

**position** (F34)          **speed** (F35)          **velocity** (F35)

**acceleration** (F35)          **momentum** (F36)

**Fill in each blank with a vocabulary term. Each term may be used more than once.**

1. When track runners finish a race, they don't just suddenly stop at the finish line. The runners' _____momentum_____ carries them well past the finish line, before they can slow down and then stop.

2. You can usually tell when an object is in motion because you can see its _____position_____ changing.

3. Some people think that _____acceleration_____ just means speeding up, but it can also mean slowing down.

4. _____Velocity_____ isn't just an object's _____speed_____, it's also the object's direction of travel.

5. Earth is moving through space. One way we can tell Earth is moving is by observing how our _____position_____ changes in relation to the stars.

6. If an object is traveling at a constant speed and then changes direction, we say its _____velocity_____ has changed. We call this change _____acceleration_____.

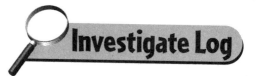
# How Mass and Velocity Affect Momentum

## Materials

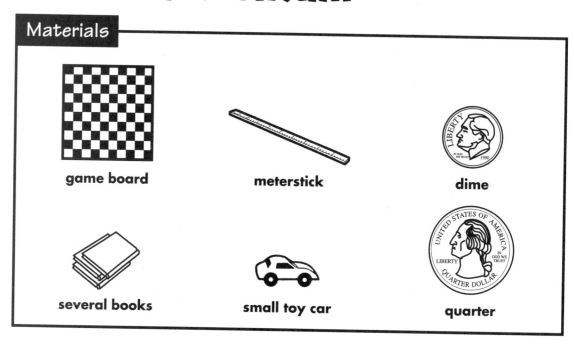

game board

meterstick

dime

several books

small toy car

quarter

## Activity Procedure

**1** Make a ramp by setting one end of the game board on a stack of books about 15 cm high. Place another book as a barrier about 10–15 cm from the bottom of the ramp.

**2** Position the car at the top of the ramp. Put the dime on one end of the car. Let the car roll down the ramp and strike the barrier. **Observe** what happens to the dime. **Measure** and **record** its distance from the barrier.

**3** Repeat Step 2, this time placing the quarter on the car instead of the dime. **Observe** what happens to the quarter. **Measure** and **record** its distance from the barrier.

**4** Repeat Steps 2 and 3 several times. **Measure** and **record** the distance for each trial.

**5** **Predict** how the results would differ if the ramp were steeper. Add another book to the stack under the ramp, and repeat Steps 2 and 3 several times. **Measure** and **record** the distances for each trial.

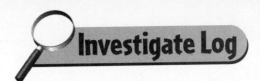
## Draw Conclusions

1. Make a table to organize your data. **Compare** the results for the dime with the results for the quarter. **Infer** how the mass of the coin is related to the distance it travels. _____ The quarter travels farther than the dime. Students should infer that the greater the coin's mass, the farther it travels.

_____

2. What happened to the distances the coins traveled when you made the ramp steeper? Explain the results. _____ Both coins traveled farther. Making the ramp steeper increases the velocity of the cart, which increases the momentum of the coins.

_____

3. **Scientists at Work** While **gathering data**, scientists try to **identify and control variables**, or conditions, that may affect the results. In this investigation, what variables did you control in Steps 2 and 3? _____ the height of the ramp (velocity of the car) and the distance the car traveled

_____

What variable did you test? _____ the size (mass) of the coin

_____

**Investigate Further** **Plan and conduct a simple investigation** to test various methods of keeping the coin on the car when it strikes the barrier. Carefully select the equipment you will need, and conduct several trials for each method you test. Students must devise a "seat belt" for the coin. Challenge them to use their results to encourage people to wear seatbelts in automobiles.

_____

_____

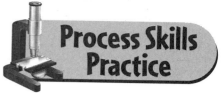

# Identify and Control Variables

When you identify and control variables, you find out which conditions in an experiment make a difference in the outcome. Controlling variables means changing one condition while keeping all the other conditions the same.

## Think About Identifying and Controlling Variables

Ann and Barbara decide to ride their bicycles from their houses to the park. Ann claims that her bicycle is faster than Barbara's, and that therefore, she will get to the park first. They both live the same distance from the park. The road from Ann's house is paved. The road from Barbara's house is dirt and gravel. Ann takes off her coat before she rides. Barbara likes the sound of her coat flapping in the wind, so she leaves her coat on. The two of them race from their separate houses, and Ann wins. Did she win because her bicycle is faster?

1. Was the race a fair test of which bicycle is faster? Explain. _____
   _____
   _____

2. What were some variables in the race? _____
   _____

3. Which condition was the same? In other words, which variable was controlled?
   _____

4. Which variables were not controlled? _____
   _____

5. What would be a good way of testing the hypothesis that Ann's bicycle is faster than Barbara's? _____
   _____
   _____
   _____
   _____
   _____

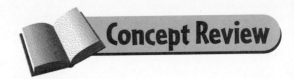
**Concept Review**

# What Are the Three Laws of Motion?

## Lesson Concept

The first law of motion is that an object at rest tends to remain at rest and an object in motion tends to move in a straight line at a constant speed, unless an outside force acts on it. The second law is that an object's acceleration depends on the mass of the object and on the size and direction of the force acting on it. The third law is that for every action, there is an equal and opposite reaction.

## Vocabulary

| **inertia** (F41) | **action force** (F43) | **reaction force** (F43) |

Write *true* in front of the true statements and *false* in front of the false statements. If the statement is false, write a correction in the space provided.

___true___ **1.** The same force that causes a pencil to fall to the floor also causes the moon to orbit Earth. _____

___true___ **2.** A moving object tends to continue moving in a straight line unless something pushes or pulls it out of its path. _____

_____

___false___ **3.** The inertia of an object depends directly on its motion.
The inertia of an object depends directly on its mass.

___true___ **4.** Newton's first law of motion explains why when you are riding in a car, you feel forced outward, away from the direction of turns.

_____

___false___ **5.** An action force makes a rocket move. A reaction force makes a rocket move.

___true___ **6.** Newton's second law of motion explains how an unbalanced force on an object causes it to accelerate. _____

_____

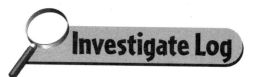
# Orbits and Inertia

## Materials

**2-m string**

**safety goggles**

**metal washers**

### CAUTION  Activity Procedure

**1** Tie three or four metal washers securely to one end of the string.

**2** **CAUTION** **Take the string with the washers outside to an open area. Be sure that you are far from any buildings or objects and that no one is standing close to you. Put on the safety goggles.** Hold the loose end of the string. Slowly swing the string and washers in a circle above your head. **Observe** the motion of the washers.

**3** **Predict** what will happen if you let go of the string while swinging it in a circle.

**4** **CAUTION** **Again, make sure that there are no people, buildings, or other objects near you.** Swing the string and washers in a circle again. Let the string slip through your fingers. **Observe** the motion of the washers. How does it **compare** with your prediction?

**5** Using a drawing, **record** the motion of the washers in Steps 2 and 4. Be sure to show the forces acting in each situation. Now make a drawing of the moon orbiting Earth. **Compare** the two drawings.

Name _____

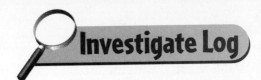

## Draw Conclusions

1. **Compare** the path of the washers while you were swinging them with their path once you let go of the string. While the student swings the string, the washers move in a circular path because of the force exerted by the string. When the string is let go, the washers fly off in a straight line because of inertia.

2. The string and washers can be used to **model** the moon orbiting Earth. **Compare** the motion of the washers circling your head with the motion of the moon orbiting Earth. Inertia keeps the washers and the moon moving. The force exerted by the string keeps the motion of the washers circular, while gravitation keeps the moon orbiting Earth.

3. **Scientists at Work** When scientists **experiment**, they must **communicate** their results to others. One way of doing this is with diagrams. Look at the drawing you made of the washers. What motions and forces does it show? Student diagrams should show the circular and straight-line motions of the washers. They should also show the force exerted by the string on the washers and the force exerted by the washers on the string.

**Investigate Further Hypothesize** about the effect the length of the string has on the time the washers take to complete one revolution. Then **experiment** to test your hypothesis. _____

_____

_____

_____

Name _____

Date _____

# Communicate

When you communicate in science, you are showing the results of an activity, such as an experiment, in an organized fashion so that the results can be interpreted later. If you communicate well, you or someone else can repeat the experiment to demonstrate it to others, or you can build on the work to make further discoveries.

## Think About Communicating

In the 1600s a mathematician named Johannes Kepler was given an assignment to analyze records of the motions of the planets to figure out the nature of their orbits. This was before telescopes, before Newton's laws of motion, and at a time when people knew very little about the planets. The records he studied had been kept very carefully by an astronomer named Tycho Brahe (TEE•koh BRAH•hee) and were considered very accurate. After studying the data, Kepler was able to describe the orbits of Mars and Earth as ellipses. He used this new information to figure out three laws of planetary motion, and he published his findings in two books. A few years afterward, a young scientist named Isaac Newton used the information communicated by Johannes Kepler to figure out the law of universal gravitation.

1. What kind of communication enabled Kepler to reach his conclusions?

   _____

2. How did Kepler communicate his own discoveries? _____

3. Kepler's books described the orbits of planets. If you were helping him write his books, how would you suggest he communicate his findings?

   _____

   _____

   _____

4. Part of effective scientific communication is making sure others will understand the information you are sharing. Do you think Brahe's scientific

   communication was effective? Was Kepler's? Explain. _____

   _____

   _____

   _____

Name _____

Date _____

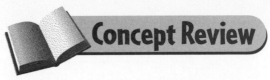

# Why Do the Planets Stay in Orbit?

## Lesson Concept

The moon circles Earth in a path called an orbit. Gravitation between Earth and the moon keeps the moon from flying off into space because of its inertia. The balance between inertia and gravitation keeps Earth in orbit around the sun. It also keeps other planets and moons in their orbits.

## Vocabulary

**orbit** (F48)                    **law of universal gravitation** (F49)

**Answer each question with one or more complete sentences.**

**1.** If Earth suddenly disappeared, the moon would no longer be under its gravitational influence. Would the moon then fly off in a straight line? Explain. No; because it would still be under the influence of the sun's gravitation, the moon would continue to orbit the sun.

**2.** Newton's law of universal gravitation says that all objects in the universe are attracted to all other objects. You already know this means that the moon is attracted toward Earth. Does the law of universal gravitation also mean that Earth is attracted toward the moon? Explain. Yes; the moon is also an object with a huge mass and therefore pulls Earth toward it.

**3.** Gravitational force decreases with distance. What does this mean for a space traveler who leaves Earth in a spaceship? As you travel away from Earth in a spaceship, the farther away you get, the less you feel the pull of Earth's gravitation.

**4.** As you travel through space away from Earth, what does the universal law of gravitation say about objects you may encounter that have huge masses ? You will be attracted to them as you were attracted to Earth when you were closer to it.

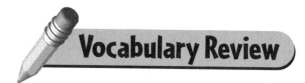
# Recognize Vocabulary

Use the following terms to solve the crossword puzzle.

| | | |
|---|---|---|
| position | speed | velocity |
| acceleration | momentum | inertia |
| action force | reaction force | orbit |
| law of universal gravitation | | |

**Across**

2. a measure of the distance an object travels in a certain length of time
6. the force that pushes or pulls back in response to another force
7. an object's speed in a particular direction
8. any change in velocity
9. a force that acts on an object
10. the property that resists any change in an object's motion

**Down**

1. an object's place or location
3. a measure of how hard it is to slow down or stop an object
4. If you say that everything is attracted to everything else, you are stating the law of universal ____.
5. the path an object in space takes as it revolves around another object

Chapter 3 • Graphic Organizer for Chapter Concepts

Forms of Energy

# Changing Energy Forms

## Materials

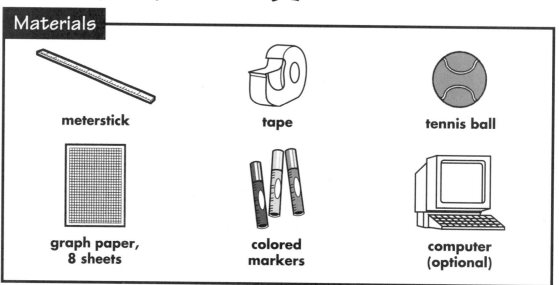

**meterstick**

**tape**

**tennis ball**

**graph paper, 8 sheets**

**colored markers**

**computer (optional)**

## Activity Procedure

**1** Tape four sheets of graph paper vertically to a wall. Starting at the floor, use the meterstick to mark off 10-cm intervals on the left edge of the paper to a height of 100 cm.

**2** Work with a partner. One person sits on the floor about 0.5 m from the graph paper. The other person holds the tennis ball a few centimeters from the wall at the 50-cm mark. Then he or she drops the ball.

**3** The seated person **observes** the ball as it bounces, and uses a colored marker to **record** the height of each bounce on the graph paper. **Count** and record the number of times the ball bounces.

**4** Repeat Steps 2 and 3 several times. Use a different-colored marker to **record** each trial.

**5** Replace the paper and repeat Steps 1–4, but this time drop the ball from a height of 100 cm.

Name _____

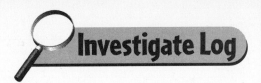 

## Draw Conclusions

**1. Compare** the drop height to the bounce height for each trial in the experiment. How are the heights related? _The higher the drop height, the higher the_ _bounce height._

_____

**2.** When you hold the ball in the air before dropping it, it has *potential energy* because of its position and because of gravitation. When you let go of the ball, it has *kinetic energy* because of its movement. **Infer** the point at which the ball has the most kinetic energy. _at its point of greatest speed—just before it hits_ _the floor for the first time._

_____

**3. Draw a conclusion** about how potential energy and kinetic energy are related in the bouncing ball. _They are inversely related; as kinetic energy increases,_ _potential energy decreases._

_____

**4. Scientists at Work** Scientists often use computers to help them **interpret data** and **communicate** the results of an experiment. Use a computer graphing program, such as *Graph Links*, to **compare** the height of each bounce and the number of bounces from one trial of the 50-cm drops and one trial of the 100-cm drops. Make a different-colored line graph for each trial.

_____

_____

_____

**Investigate Further** Analyze the data you graphed in Step 4 and **predict** how high and how many times a ball dropped from a height of 200 cm will bounce. Then **experiment** and **compare** your results to your predictions.

_____

_____

_____

_____

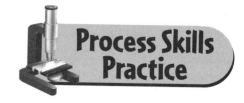

Process Skills
Practice

# Communicate

When you communicate, you transmit data or information to others. You can use spoken or written words, graphs, drawings, diagrams, maps, and charts to communicate. Communicating in science means showing the results of an activity in an organized fashion so that the data can be interpreted or the activity repeated.

## Think About Communicating

Here is some data from an experiment to observe the potential and kinetic energy of a basketball.

Dropped from 1 meter. Trial 1: Bounced 60 cm. Trial 2: Bounced 70 cm. Trial 3: Bounced 80 cm.

Dropped from 2 meters. Trial 1: Bounced 1 m 40 cm. Trial 2: Bounced 1 m 25 cm. Trial 3: Bounced 1 m 40 cm.

**Communicate these results on the graphs.**

Name _____

Date _____

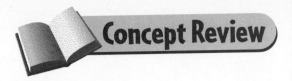

# What Are Kinetic and Potential Energy?

## Lesson Concept

Energy is the ability to cause changes in matter. There are two basic types of energy—kinetic energy and potential energy. Kinetic and potential energy can be found in many forms. Electric energy, thermal energy, mechanical energy, light, and sound are all forms of kinetic energy. Chemical potential energy, gravitational potential energy, and elastic potential energy are forms of potential energy. The law of conservation of energy says energy can change form but cannot be created or destroyed.

## Vocabulary

| | | |
|---|---|---|
| **energy** (F62) | **kinetic energy** (F62) | **potential energy** (F62) |

Decide whether the underlined term or phrase makes each statement true or false. If the statement is true, write the word *true* on the line. If the statement is false, write a word or phrase that makes the statement true.

_____true_____ **1.** Energy is the <u>ability to do work</u>.

_____true_____ **2.** The energy of motion is called <u>kinetic energy</u>.

_____true_____ **3.** The energy an object has because of where it is or because of its condition is called <u>potential energy</u>.

_____kinetic_____ **4.** A boulder rolling down a hill has <u>potential</u> energy.

_____kinetic_____ **5.** Mechanical energy is a form of <u>potential</u> energy.

_____can change_____ **6.** Energy <u>never changes</u> from one form to another during any one activity.

_____kinetic_____ **7.** Thermal energy and light energy are two forms of <u>potential</u> energy.

_____true_____ **8.** An apple that is ready to drop from the tree to the ground has gravitational <u>potential</u> energy.

_____potential_____ **9.** The energy stored in a compressed spring is called elastic <u>kinetic</u> energy.

**Use with page F65.**

# Electric Circuits

## Materials

**4 lengths of insulated wire with bare ends**

**2 light bulb holders**

**battery**

**2 light bulbs**

**battery holder**

## Activity Procedure

**1** To make electricity flow between the terminals, or charged ends, of a dry cell or battery, you need to connect the terminals in some way, such as with a wire. Electricity will then flow through any device you put along this path. Connect the wires, bulb holders, and battery holder as shown in Picture A on page F67.

**2** Insert the light bulbs and batteries. **Observe** what happens and **record** your observations.

**3** Remove one of the bulbs from its holder. **Observe** and **record** what happens to the other bulb.

**4** Now reconnect the wires, bulb holders, and battery holder as shown in Picture B on page F67. **Observe** what happens and **record** your observations.

**5** Again remove one of the bulbs from its holder. **Observe** and **record** what happens to the other bulb.

**6** Draw diagrams of both of the circuits you built. Use arrows to **compare** the path of the electric current in each circuit.

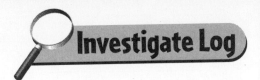
**Investigate Log**

## Draw Conclusions

1. What happened to the other bulb when one bulb was removed from the first circuit? It went out. _____

2. What happened to the other bulb when one bulb was removed from the second circuit? It stayed on. _____

3. **Scientists at Work** Scientists often **compare** results before they **draw a conclusion**. Cross out one bulb in each of your drawings. Then diagram the path the electric current must take if it can't pass through the bulb you crossed out. Compare your diagrams, and then draw a conclusion about which type of circuit would be better to use for a string of lights. The second circuit would be better because one burned-out bulb wouldn't stop the electricity from reaching the other bulbs. _____

_____

_____

**Investigate Further** In the investigation you demonstrated that electricity flowing through a circuit produces light and heat (the glowing bulbs were warm). Now **plan and conduct a simple investigation** to demonstrate that electricity flowing through a circuit can also produce sound and magnetism. Decide what equipment you will need to use in your investigation. _____

_____

_____

_____

_____

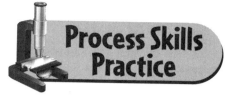
Process Skills
Practice

# Compare and Draw Conclusions

When you compare, you identify common and distinguishing characteristics of objects or events. When you draw a conclusion, you pull together all that you have discovered in observing, researching, and investigating.

## Think About Comparing and Drawing Conclusions

Comparing the characteristics of different things is a good way to learn those characteristics and draw conclusions about them. Look at the data in the chart below and then answer the questions that follow.

| | Materials That Allow Electricity to Flow | Materials That Do Not Allow Electricity to Flow |
|---|---|---|
| Porous | watery substances, salt solutions, acid solutions | Leather, cotton, wool, parchment, ashes, chalk, hair, feathers, wood |
| Nonporous | iron, copper, silver, graphite, charcoal | rubber, porcelain, vinyl, plastics, precious stones, ceramic, glass, resin, amber |

1. When you plug something into an electrical outlet, you don't want electricity to flow from the wires into your hand. The plug must therefore be made of material that does not allow electricity to flow. Compare the properties of the materials listed in the chart. Draw a conclusion about which materials would be good for making plugs. _____

   _____

2. Explain why you chose those materials. _____

   _____

   _____

   _____

3. List two materials that would be good to use for wires to carry electricity in a circuit and explain why. _____

   _____

Name _____

Date _____

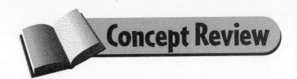 **Concept Review**

# What Is Electric Energy?

## Lesson Concept

Electric energy is the movement of electrons between areas that have opposite charges. When objects with opposite charges are close enough together or when the charges are very large, electrons move between the objects. Electric current moves through an electric circuit. When electric current flows through a conductor, it produces a magnetic field, turning the conductor into an electromagnet.

## Vocabulary

**electric charge** (F68)      **electric force** (F69)      **electric current** (F69)

**conductor** (F70)      **electric circuit** (F71)      **insulator** (F71)

**resistor** (F71)      **electromagnet** (F72)

**Match the term in the left column with its description in the right column.**

___D___ **1.** positive charge

___F___ **2.** static electricity

___I___ **3.** series circuit

___G___ **4.** proton

___A___ **5.** electric energy

___H___ **6.** electric current

___J___ **7.** conductor

___K___ **8.** generator

___B___ **9.** electron

___L___ **10.** resistor

___E___ **11.** electric force

___C___ **12.** negative charge

**A** the energy produced by the movement of electrons

**B** an atomic particle with a negative charge

**C** the charge an object has when it has gained electrons

**D** the charge an object has when it has lost electrons

**E** the attraction or repulsion that unlike or like charges have

**F** the potential electric energy of a charged object

**G** an atomic particle with a positive charge

**H** the flow of electrons

**I** a circuit with only one path for the electrons

**J** a material that carries electrons easily

**K** a source of electrons

**L** a material that resists electric current

**Use with page F73.**

Workbook   WB257

Name _____

Date _____

# The Path of Reflected Light

## Materials

ruler

small mirror

protractor

piece of corrugated cardboard, 10 cm × 10 cm

masking tape

3 pushpins of different colors

## Activity Procedure

**1** Lay the cardboard flat. Use the tape to attach the mirror vertically to one end of the cardboard. Push two of the pins into the cardboard, about 5 cm from the mirror.

**2** Position yourself at eye level with the mirror. Align yourself so that your view of one pin lines up with the reflection of the other pin. Push a third pin into the cardboard at the edge of the mirror, right in front of where you see the reflection of the second pin. The first pin, the third pin, and the reflection of the second pin should appear to be in a straight line.

**3** Draw lines on the cardboard to connect the three pins. These lines show how the reflected light from the first pin traveled to your eye.

**4** Using the protractor, **measure** the angle between each line and the edge of the mirror. You will probably have to trace the edge of the mirror and then move it out of your way to make this measurement. **Record** your results.

**5** Now remove the original pins and place two of them 10 cm from the mirror. Repeat Steps 2–4 with this new arrangement of pins. **Measure** the angles of the new lines, and **record** your results.

Name _____

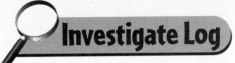

**6** Now draw diagrams to **communicate** the results of the two experiments. Each diagram should show the locations of the pins and the mirror and the path of the reflected light.

## Draw Conclusions

**1. Compare** the two angles you **measured** in each experiment.

The two angles should be congruent in each case.

_____

_____

**2.** The angle at which light strikes a mirror is the *angle of incidence*. The angle at which it reflects from the mirror is the *angle of reflection*. **Draw a conclusion** about the angle of incidence and the angle of reflection from a flat surface.

The angle of incidence and the angle of reflection have the same

measurement.

_____

**3. Scientists at Work** When scientists **observe** a pattern that seems to always be true, they try to come up with a clear, simple rule. This helps them **predict** what will happen in the future. Predict what the angle of incidence and the angle of reflection would be if the pins were 20 cm from the mirror.

Students should predict that the angles will still be congruent.

_____

**Investigate Further Hypothesize** how light would be reflected from a mirror that was not flat. Then **plan and conduct a simple investigation** to test your hypothesis.

_____

_____

_____

_____

Name _____

Date _____

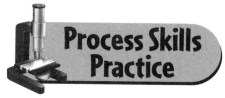

# Predict

When you predict, you anticipate outcomes of future events, basing your ideas on your prior experience, observations, or knowledge.

## Think About Predicting

Louise was given a toy guitar for her birthday. She noticed that plucking on the thicker strings made a sound lower in pitch than the sound made by plucking on the thinner strings. She also noticed that if she tightened a string, the sound it produced would become higher in pitch. She also noticed that all the strings on her mother's guitar produced sounds lower in pitch than the strings on her toy guitar. She observed that all the strings on her mother's guitar were longer than the strings on her toy guitar.

Louise inferred from her observations that the thinner, the shorter, or the tighter the string, the higher the pitch of its sound. She thought she could use this inference to predict the sounds that other stringed instruments would make.

**1.** What is Louise trying to predict? _____

_____

**2.** What information does she have that will help her predict? _____

_____

**3.** A cello is a stringed instrument that looks like a very large violin. What could Louise predict about the sounds that a cello might make? Explain.

_____

_____

**4.** Louise knew that a piano is a stringed instrument. What could she predict about the strings that would be hammered when she played the keys that

produce low-pitched sounds? _____

_____

**5.** If you used Louise's observations, what could you predict about the sounds different-sized drums might make? Explain your answer by using Louise's

inference. _____

_____

_____

**Use with page F75.**

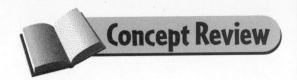

**Concept Review**

# What Are Light and Sound Energy?

## Lesson Concept

Light energy is electromagnetic energy that travels through space and through certain materials. When light waves strike an obstacle, they are absorbed, reflected, or refracted. Lenses are curved pieces of transparent matter that refract light rays. Sound energy is vibrations that travel through matter. Solids and liquids conduct sound better than gases.

## Vocabulary

**reflection** (F76)        **refraction** (F76)        **lens** (F77)

**pitch** (F79)        **volume** (F79)

**Choose the answer that best completes each statement.**

**1.** A _____ lens is thicker in the middle than at the edges.
   **A** concave        **B** convex        **C** reflection

**2.** The bending of light rays is called _____
   **A** reflection        **B** absorption        **C** refraction

**3.** When light rays bounce off an object, the bouncing is called _____
   **A** absorption        **B** refraction        **C** reflection

**4.** The colors of light that objects _____ are the colors we see.
   **A** absorb        **B** reflect        **C** refract

**5.** Sound waves have two parts, compression and _____
   **A** rarefaction        **B** refraction        **C** reflection

**6.** Light energy moves as waves called _____
   **A** magnetic waves        **B** vibrating waves        **C** electromagnetic waves

**7.** The _____ is the colored part of the eye that narrows and widens to control the amount of light entering the eye.
   **A** pupil        **B** iris        **C** cornea

Name _____

Date _____

# Heat Flow

## Materials

margarine

Styrofoam cup

clock

metal butter knife

hot water

plastic knife

 CAUTION  ## Activity Procedure

1. Place a dab of cold margarine near the middle of the metal knife. Place another dab of margarine the same size near the tip of the knife's blade.

2. **CAUTION** **Be careful when pouring the hot water.** Half-fill the cup with hot water. Put the metal knife's handle into the water. The dabs of margarine should be above the level of the water.

3. **Predict** which dab of margarine will melt first—the one near the middle of the knife or the one near the end of the knife.

4. **Observe** the metal knife for ten minutes and **record** your observations.

5. Repeat Steps 1–4 using the plastic knife.

6. **Experiment** to find out which material transfers heat faster—metal or plastic. Be sure to **identify and control variables** that might affect the results.

Name _____

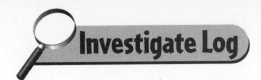
Investigate Log

## Draw Conclusions

**1. Draw conclusions** about how heat moves through the metal knife.

Heat moves from one end of the knife to the other, since the margarine near

the middle of the knife melted first.

_____

**2. Draw conclusions** about which material transfers heat faster.

Metal transfers heat faster.

_____

**3. Scientists at Work** Scientists must **identify and control variables** in an experiment to see how changing one variable affects the results. What variables did you control in your experiment? What variable did you test?

Controlled variables should include the lengths of the knives and

temperatures and amounts of both the margarine and the water.

The only variable that should change is the material through which the

heat is transferred.

_____

**Investigate Further  Experiment** to find out which knife cools faster. Decide what equipment you will need. _____

_____

_____

_____

Name _____

Date _____

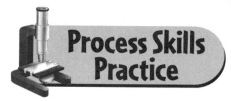

# Identify and Control Variables

When you identify and control variables that affect the outcome of an experiment, you state which factors could affect the outcome of the experiment and you make sure that only one of those factors, or variables, is changed in any given test.

## Think About Identifying and Controlling Variables

Suppose you are an architect trying to design an energy-efficient house. You want to know which wall and ceiling insulating materials work best so the house can be cooled and heated as inexpensively as possible. You also want lots of windows in the house so you can take advantage of natural light during the day. Windows, however, are where a house loses most of its warmed or cooled interior air. So you want windows that are good insulators but still allow light to pass through freely. You have a choice of three wall and ceiling insulating materials, and you have a choice of two window materials. You decide to build several small buildings the size and shape of doghouses for your test.

**1.** What are you testing? _____

_____

**2.** What are some variables in your tests? _____

_____

_____

_____

_____

_____

_____

**3.** Which of the variables will you control? _____

_____

_____

**4.** Will using doghouse-sized models give you accurate results? Explain.

_____

_____

_____

_____

**Use with page F83**

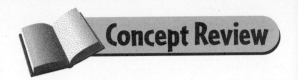
Concept Review

# What Are Thermal and Chemical Energy?

## Lesson Concept

Thermal energy is the kinetic energy of molecules. The average kinetic energy of the molecules in an object is the object's temperature. Heat is the transfer of thermal energy from one object to another. Conduction is the direct transfer of heat between objects that touch. Convection is the transfer of heat through currents in a gas or a liquid. Radiation is the transfer of energy by electromagnetic waves. When atoms join to form molecules, thermal energy can be stored as chemical energy. Chemical energy can be released as kinetic energy.

## Vocabulary

| | | |
|---|---|---|
| **temperature** (F84) | **heat** (F84) | **conduction** (F85) |
| **convection** (F85) | **radiation** (F85) | |

**Fill in each blank with a vocabulary term. You may use each term more than once.**

1. When you add _____heat_____ to an object, you increase the kinetic energy of the object's molecules, which increases its _____temperature_____.

2. If you leave a metal stirring spoon in a pot of soup while the soup is heating, the spoon will quickly get hot because of _____conduction_____.

3. When you sit near a campfire, the heat of the fire is transferred to you mostly by _____radiation_____.

4. If your house is heated by a furnace that blows hot air into the rooms, you are depending on the process of _____convection_____ to stay warm.

5. A lizard sometimes stretches out on a rock to warm itself. The rock is warm because the sun has transferred thermal energy to it by _____radiation_____. The rock then transfers thermal energy to the lizard by _____conduction_____. The rock also transfers thermal energy to air above it and the lizard through a process called _____convection_____.

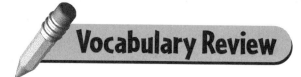
**Vocabulary Review**

# Recognize Vocabulary

Write the letter of the definition in the right column next to the
term that it matches in the left column.

_____ **1.** conductor

_____ **2.** temperature

_____ **3.** electric circuit

_____ **4.** lens

_____ **5.** electric current

_____ **6.** convection

_____ **7.** potential energy

_____ **8.** heat

_____ **9.** insulator

_____ **10.** electric charge

_____ **11.** pitch

_____ **12.** electromagnet

_____ **13.** refraction

_____ **14.** energy

_____ **15.** electric force

_____ **16.** radiation

_____ **17.** conduction

_____ **18.** resistor

_____ **19.** volume

_____ **20.** reflection

_____ **21.** Kinetic energy

**A** a magnet formed by the flow of electric current

**B** energy of motion

**C** a material that doesn't carry electrons

**D** what an object gets when it gains or loses electrons

**E** the loudness of a sound

**F** the average kinetic energy of all the molecules in an object

**G** the transfer of thermal energy by electromagnetic waves

**H** energy an object has because of its condition

**I** a quality determined by the speed of vibration of sound waves

**J** a material that conducts electrons easily

**K** light that bounces off an object

**L** the attraction or repulsion between objects with a positive or negative charge

**M** the direct transfer of thermal energy between objects that touch

**N** the bending of light rays

**O** the ability to cause changes in matter

**P** the flow of electrons

**Q** the transfer of thermal energy from one substance to another

**R** a piece of clear material that bends light rays passing through it

**S** the transfer of thermal energy through currents in a liquid or a gas

**T** a material that resists the flow of electrons

**U** any path along which electrons can flow

# Chapter 4 • Graphic Organizer for Chapter Concepts

## How People Use Energy

# How Stored Energy Is Released

## Materials

| | | | |
|---|---|---|---|
| water | measuring cup | Styrofoam cup | thermometer |
| clock with second hand | safety goggles | calcium chloride | spoon |

**CAUTION**

## Activity Procedure

**1** Use the table on the next page for this activity. Measure 50 mL of water in the measuring cup, and pour it into the Styrofoam cup. Put the thermometer in the water. After 30 seconds, **measure** the temperature of the water and **record** it in the table.

**2** **CAUTION** Put on the safety goggles. Add 2 spoonfuls of calcium chloride to the cup of water. Stir the water with the spoon until the calcium chloride dissolves. Wait 30 seconds. Then **measure** and **record** the temperature.

**3** **Measure** and **record** the temperature of the water two more times, after 60 seconds and after 120 seconds. Then **compare** the temperature of the water before and after you added calcium chloride.

| Substance | Temperature |
|---|---|
| Water without chemical | |
| Water with chemical after 30 seconds | |
| Water with chemical after 60 seconds | |
| Water with chemical after 120 seconds | |

## Draw Conclusions

1. How did the temperature of the water change when you added calcium chloride? The temperature increased.

2. **Infer** whether the calcium chloride gives off heat or absorbs heat as it dissolves in water. It gives off heat as it dissolves.

3. What do you **infer** might have caused the water temperature to change? Possible answer: As the calcium chloride reacted with the water, chemical bonds were broken and heat was given off.

4. **Scientists at Work** Scientists **observe** and **measure** to gather as much data as they can from an experiment. What did you learn from this experiment about how the chemical energy in some compounds can be released? The chemical energy in some compounds can be released by dissolving the compounds in water. The energy is released as heat.

**Investigate Further** **Hypothesize** what will happen when a different chemical, such as magnesium sulfate (Epsom salts), is placed in water. Then **plan and conduct a simple investigation** to test your hypothesis. _____

_____

Name _____

Date _____

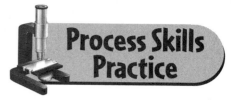

# Observe and Measure

When you observe, you use one or more of your senses to perceive properties of objects and events. One type of observing is measuring. When you measure, you are making observations with the aid of instruments, such as stopwatches or thermometers.

## Think About Observing and Measuring

Before you can effectively measure anything, you have to know what you will be measuring. Then you choose the appropriate instrument for the type of measuring you will be doing. In the following questions, you will be asked to make those decisions.

1. You are working for a veterinarian. It is your job to feed the dogs. Your instructions are to feed each dog twice a day, one-half cup at each feeding for every 15 pounds that the dog weighs. What observations will you be making,

   and what measuring instruments will you be using? _____

   _____

   _____

2. You are part of a mapping expedition that is going into unexplored territory. The expedition plans to take a boat up the river until it reaches the river's source. Your job is to map the course of the river for later expeditions. What observations will you make? What instruments and what units of measure will

   you use? _____

   _____

   _____

   _____

3. A local television station has asked you to be part of a weather watch. They expect you to call the station every day at 4:00 P.M. and tell them the temperature, sky conditions, the wind speed, and any other observation you think might be important. What will you be observing and what instruments will you use?

   _____

   _____

   _____

   _____

Use with page F97.

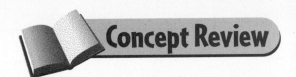

Concept Review

# How Do People Use Fossil Fuels?

## Lesson Concept

Coal, natural gas, and petroleum are fossil fuels formed from once-living matter that has been buried for millions of years. Fossil fuels are used to heat homes, move cars, and generate electricity. Because fossil fuels take millions of years to form, they are nonrenewable.

## Vocabulary

**chemical bonds** (F98)

**Answer each question with one or more complete sentences.**

**1.** How did energy from sunlight become stored in fossil fuels?

Fossil fuels are the remains of once-living things. The living things stored

energy from the sun in the chemical bonds of their molecules.

**2.** How does burning fuel of any kind turn solar energy into thermal energy?

Solar energy is stored as chemical energy in living things. The fuel is made

of material that used to be one or many living things. Burning the fuel turns

the chemical energy into thermal energy by breaking chemical bonds.

**3.** Why are fossil fuels the main source of energy for so many people?

They release more energy when they are burned than other fuels.

**4.** Where is most of the chemical energy in living organisms stored?

It is stored mostly in chemical bonds that join carbon atoms to each other

and to atoms of hydrogen and other elements.

**5.** What type of fossil fuel is the main source of energy for transportation?

Petroleum is the main source of energy for transportation.

**6.** Give at least two reasons other sources of energy besides fossil fuels should be used. Fossil fuels are nonrenewable resources; they are needed to make

new materials such as plastics; burning fossil fuels releases large amounts of

carbon dioxide into the air.

# Water Power

## Materials

two 10-cm plastic disks

stapler

scissors

pencil sharpened at both ends

0.5-m length of string

30-g mass

basin

1-L plastic bottle filled with water

meterstick

stopwatch

**CAUTION**

## Activity Procedure

1. **CAUTION** Be careful when using the scissors. Staple the plastic disks together near their centers. Using the scissors, cut four 3-cm slits into the disks as shown on page F103. At each slit, fold the disks in opposite directions to form a vane.

2. Again using the scissors, punch a 0.5-cm hole at the center of the disks. Insert the pencil. It will serve as the axle on which the water wheel rotates.

3. Use the scissors to make a smaller hole next to the pencil hole. Insert one end of the string into the hole, and tie a knot in the string to keep it in place. Tie the mass to the other end of the string.

4. Place the basin near the edge of the desk. Hold your water wheel over the basin. Your fingertips should hold the pencil points so the pencil can turn. The mass on the string should hang over the edge of the desk.

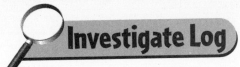

**Investigate Log**

**5** Have a partner slowly pour water over the wheel from a height of about 10 cm. Using the stopwatch, **measure** and **record** the time it takes for the mass to reach the level of the desk. Repeat this step several times.

**6** Now repeat Steps 4 and 5, but have your partner pour the water from a height of about 20 cm. Again, **measure** and **record** the time it takes for the mass to reach the level of the desk.

## Draw Conclusions

1. What **variables** did you **control** in your investigation? _the amount of water_
_in the bottle and the rate at which the water was poured_

What variable did you change? _the height from which the water fell_

_____

2. Recall that the greater the power, the more quickly work is done. Which of your trials produced more power? Why? _the trial in which the water fell from the_
_greater height, because work was done more quickly during this trial_

3. **Scientists at Work** Scientists often look beyond the results of an investigation. For example, how does the height from which the water is poured affect the speed at which the water wheel turns? **Plan and conduct a simple investigation** to find out. Be sure to **identify and control variables**, changing only the height from which the water falls. _Students should hypothesize_
_that increasing the height from which the water falls produces more force,_
_which turns the wheel faster. Investigations should confirm this hypothesis._

_____

**Investigate Further Hypothesize** about the rate of flow and the speed at which the water wheel turns. Then **plan and conduct a simple investigation** to test your hypothesis. Be sure to **identify and control variables**, changing only the rate of flow of the water. _____

_____

_____

Name _____

Date _____

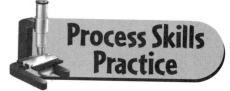

# Identify and Control Variables

Identifying and controlling variables involves stating or controlling factors that affect the outcome of an experiment. It is important that only one variable be altered in any given test.

## Think About Identifying and Controlling Variables

**Read the descriptions of the experiments below. Then identify the variables that affect the outcome of each experiment.**

1. People noticed that the number of a certain type of fish that live in a river seemed to have decreased since a dam was built on the river. Scientists who were concerned about the situation captured some of the fish and put them in giant tanks to study them. Both tanks were filled with river water. Plants, rocks, and insects from the river were also introduced into each tank. In one tank the water was 8 meters deep, the average depth of the undammed river. The water in the other tank was 30 meters deep, the depth of the river behind the dam. What is the variable in this experiment, and what could scientists learn by controlling it?

   The variable is the depth of the river. By controlling it, scientists might learn of the increased depth of the water on the declining river is harming fish.

2. Many fish died in both tanks in the investigation in Question 1. Trying to determine the cause of the fish deaths, the scientists set up two tanks each with 8 meters of water in them. New fish were introduced, along with stones, insects, and plants from the river. One tank was lit by light that simulated sunshine. The other was kept dark. What is the variable in this experiment, and what could scientists learn by controlling it? The variable is sunlight. The scientists could find out whether fish were dying because they weren't getting enough sunshine in the deep channel.

3. Patricia built two water wheels by placing a dozen plastic slats between two plastic coffee-can lids. On one water wheel, she placed the slats so they pointed straight to the center from the edge of the lids. On the other wheel, she placed the slats so they were tilted at a sharp angle from the edge of the coffee-can lids. Using a pencil as the axle, she suspended each wheel over a basin and asked an assistant to pour water over them at a steady rate from 10 centimeters above the wheel. What is the variable in Patricia's experiment, and what could she learn by controlling it? The variable is the angle of the slats. She could learn which design allows the wheel to turn more quickly.

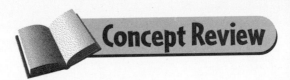

# How Can Moving Water Generate Electricity?

## Lesson Concept

An electric generator changes mechanical energy to electric energy. One source of this mechanical energy is moving water. Hydroelectric energy stations use the energy of falling water to spin turbines that generate electricity. The mechanical energy present in ocean tides can also generate electric energy.

## Vocabulary

**hydroelectric energy** (F104)     **tidal energy** (F106)

**Write a phrase from the chart to complete each sentence .**

| |
|---|
| hydroelectric energy can be traced back to the sun |
| the potential energy of water under pressure |
| by holding back water at high tide and letting it fall through turbines at low tide |
| of falling water to spin turbines that generate electricity |
| to electric energy |
| the turbine spins the shaft of an electric generator |
| can also generate electric energy |

**1.** An electric generator changes mechanical energy _to electric energy_ .

**2.** The energy that spins a hydroelectric turbine comes from _the potential energy of water under pressure_ .

**3.** Hydroelectric energy stations use the energy _of falling water to spin turbines that generate electricity_ .

**4.** The mechanical energy present in ocean tides _can also generate electric energy_ .

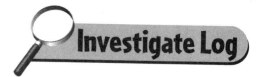
# A Steam-Powered Turbine

## Materials

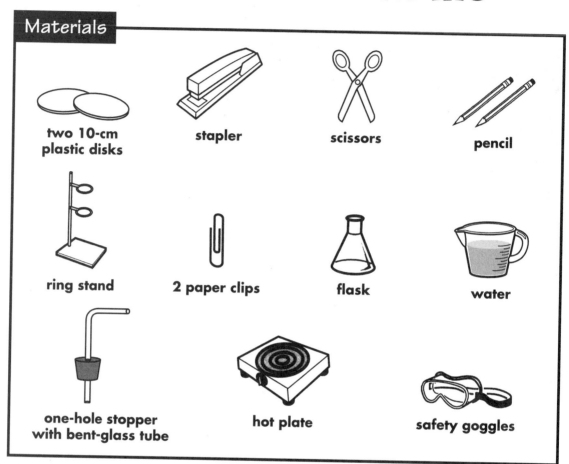

two 10-cm plastic disks

stapler

scissors

pencil

ring stand

2 paper clips

flask

water

one-hole stopper with bent-glass tube

hot plate

safety goggles

### Activity Procedure

**1** You can modify the water wheel you made in the last investigation by adding 12 more vanes to the wheel and enlarging the hole. Or you can follow Steps 2 and 3 to make your turbine.

**2** **CAUTION** **Be careful when using the scissors.** Staple the plastic disks together near their centers. Using the scissors, cut sixteen 3-cm slits into the disks as shown on page F109. At each slit, fold the disks in opposite directions to form a vane.

**3** Again using the scissors, cut a 0.5-cm round hole in the center of the disks. Make the hole as round as possible. Insert the pencil. It will serve as the axle on which the turbine rotates. The turbine should spin freely on its axle. Now suspend the axle and turbine from the ring stand arm with two bent paper clips.

❹ Fill the flask with water. Put the stopper with the bent glass tube in the flask. Set the flask on the hot plate. Point the open end of the glass tube toward the vanes on the bottom of the turbine.

❺ **CAUTION** **Put on the safety goggles, and use caution around the steam.** Turn on the hot plate. **Observe** and **record** your observations of the turbine as the water begins to boil. Draw a diagram of your turbine to **communicate** your results. Be sure to include labels and arrows to show what happens.

## Draw Conclusions

1. **Infer** the source of energy for turning the turbine. __the hot plate__

   _____

2. **Communicate** in a short paragraph how the energy from the source was changed to turn the turbine. __The water is heated by the hot plate until it__ __boils. The water turns to steam. The steam expands and is forced out of the__ __flask through the glass tube. As the steam rushes out of the glass tube, it__ __pushes against the vanes of the turbine, causing it to spin.__

3. **Scientists at Work** When scientists **communicate**, they try to show clearly or describe what is happening. In what two ways did you communicate the results of this investigation? Which way was clearer? __By writing a paragraph and by__ __drawing a diagram; the diagram may have communicated the results of the__ __investigation more clearly.__

**Investigate Further Plan and conduct a simple investigation** to determine how much work your turbine can do. Decide what questions you will need to answer and what equipment you will need to use. __Students could attach a weight on a__ __string to the turbine. By increasing the weight, they could measure about how__ __much work the turbine can do.__

# Communicate

Communicating involves the passing on of data. This may be done through spoken or written words, graphs, drawings, diagrams, maps, and charts. Communicating in science means showing the results of an activity in an organized fashion so the results can later be interpreted or the activity can be repeated.

## Think About Communicating

**In the questions below, you will find four types of information that a scientist might want to communicate. In the space provided, describe what you think would be the best way to communicate the information.**

1. A laboratory was studying the nutritional requirements of a new breed of mouse they had developed for cancer research. They discovered that the healthiest mice were those fed a diet consisting of 15 percent protein, 75 percent carbohydrates, and 10 percent fats. What sort of graph, drawing, or

   chart would best communicate these results? _____

   _____

2. A group of scientists was surveying a large open area for the placement of windmills. They wanted to be sure each windmill would receive the greatest amount of wind possible, so they placed wind vanes in the area and kept track of the wind speed and direction over a period of six months. Then they took the average for each position. What would be the best way for them to

   communicate their results? _____

   _____

3. A fisher was keeping track of the height of the tides in a certain area as part of a study being done at a local university. He drove a long measuring stick into the ground at the water's edge at low tide. Then, every hour, he checked the water's depth on the measuring stick. What kind of graphic would best

   communicate what he discovered? _____

   _____

   _____

4. Scientists were studying the relative top running speeds of animals in East Africa. They clocked a cheetah at 100 kilometers per hour (km/hr), a gazelle at 72 km/hr, a wildebeest at 36 km/hr, a leopard at 65 km/hr, and a jackal at 40 km/hr. What would be the best way to communicate this information?

   _____

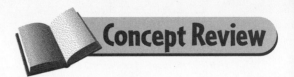
Concept Review

# What Other Sources of Energy Do People Use?

## Lesson Concept

In addition to fossil fuels and hydroelectric energy, the United States uses small amounts of energy from other sources. These sources include biomass, nuclear energy, wind, geothermal energy, and solar energy. Researchers continue to work on new sources of energy, such as fusion.

## Vocabulary

**nuclear energy** (F110)        **biomass** (F110)        **solar energy** (F111)

**fusion energy** (F112)        **geothermal energy** (F111)

List the advantages and disadvantages of each type of energy.

| Type of Energy | Advantages | Disadvantages |
|---|---|---|
| Biomass | virtually free; can be made into liquid fuel | not very efficient |
| Nuclear | produces large amount of energy from small amount of fuel | fuel and waste products very dangerous to living organisms |
| Solar | free, nonpolluting, inexhaustible | not always available; collectors and cells can be expensive |
| Wind | free, nonpolluting, inexhaustible | expensive equipment; inconstant |
| Geothermal | free, nonpolluting, inexhaustible | technology could be expensive; not available everywhere |
| Ocean Thermal | free, nonpolluting, inexhaustible | technology could be expensive; not available everywhere |
| Hydrogen | potential low cost, low risk | requires expensive energy to start process; still experimental |

Name _____

Date _____

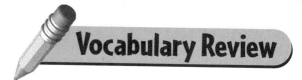

# Recognize Vocabulary

Choose one of the words from the box to answer each riddle.

| | |
|---|---|
| biomass | nuclear energy |
| hydroelectric energy | solar energy |
| geothermal energy | chemical bonds |
| fusion energy | tidal energy |

1. I'm alive now, or I was fairly recently. Burning me doesn't release a lot of energy, but I'm free or very inexpensive, so a lot of people use me. What am I?

   _____

2. I'm not a wallet, and I'm not a purse or a backpack. I'm not a bank account, but I'm the thing that all living things keep their "saved-up" energy in. What am I?

   _____

3. Look for me at Niagara Falls or Glen Canyon Dam! I'm on the Missouri River and the Tennessee River, too. What am I? _____

4. Atoms are very tiny, but if you split them apart, you'll get me, the most powerful source of thermal energy on Earth. What am I? _____

5. If you want to get your energy directly from the source, you'll come to me. Too many cloudy days, however, could make it hard for you to get enough of me. What am I? _____

6. Dig deep to find me, preferably near a volcano or an earthquake zone. What am I? _____

7. I result from something that happens twice a day. See you at the beach! What am I? _____

8. I'm in the experimental stages. Scientists know how I work, but the heat needed to get me started is so high that it burns all known materials. What am I?

   _____

**Use with pages F96–F113.**